JAZZ *Life & Times*

This is a series of books about jazz artists, all of whom have made either a significant contribution or have had an impact on the jazz scene. Unlike some jazz books that concentrate upon the detail of the performers' lives or music, this series is concerned with much more. Here can be seen the social background into which the subject was born and raised and the environment in which his or her music was formed. The social, domestic, racial and commercial pressures that shaped the person are examined alongside an assessment of other musicians who may have influenced the artist or been influenced by them. Of course, the music is not overlooked and each book carries a discographical essay in which the artist's recorded output is summarized and analyzed. Well-illustrated, the Life & Times series of books is an important and long overdue addition to jazz literature.

Gene Krupa

HIS
LIFE & TIMES

BRUCE CROWTHER

Omnibus Press

LONDON/SYDNEY/COLOGNE

In the same illustrated series:
Louis Armstrong by Mike Pinfold
Billie Holiday by John White
Bud Powell by Alan Groves

First published in Britain in 1987 by
SPELLMOUNT LTD,
Tunbridge Wells, Kent, England

This edition published in 1988 by
OMNIBUS PRESS,
a division of Book Sales Ltd.

©Bruce Crowther 1987

Exclusive distributors:
Book Sales Limited
8/9 Frith Street, London W1V 5TZ, UK.
Music Sales Pty. Limited
120 Rothschild Avenue,
Rosebery, NSW 2018, Australia.

To the Music Trade only:
Music Sales Limited
8/9 Frith Street, London, W1V 5TZ, UK.

ISBN 0-7119-1293-9
Order No. OP 444 78

Series editor: Bruce Crowther
Picture researcher: Max Jones
Designed by: Words & Images,
Speldhurst, Tunbridge Wells, Kent
Printed & bound in Great Britain by
Anchor Press Ltd, Tiptree, Essex

CONTENTS

ACKNOWLEDGEMENTS

It is a good many years since I first decided I wanted to write a book on Gene Krupa. Between that first idea and the publication of this book I have corresponded with and spoken to a great many people, some of whom I can no longer trace, and some, sadly, are no longer alive. To them all, named below or not, I wish to express my sincere gratitude. Without their contributions this book would be much less than it is.

John Christopherson, Kenny Davern, Dave Frishberg, Norman Granz, Wellington B. Holliday, Al Klopfer, Julius B. Krupa, Anders Lofquist, Don Osborne, Mike Pinfold.

The illustrations in this book come from the Max Jones Collection, the Frank Driggs Collection, Hans Harzheim, the Slingerland Drum Co, Howard Lucraft, Bengt. H. Malmqvist, Bruce Crowther and from stills used to publicize films made or distributed by the following companies: Columbia, Goldwyn, Majestic, Paramount, RKO, Universal, Warner Brothers. Record sleeves and related material from BBC, CBS, Chiaroscuro, Harold Davison, EMI, London, RCA, Swing Treasury, Verve, OKeh. Pictures are produced by courtesy of the Chicago Historical Society, Leonard Feather, *Jazz Journal International*, *Life*, Howard Lucraft, the National Film Archive, Roy Burchell and *Melody Maker*.

Although efforts have been made to trace the present copyright holders of photographs, the publishers apologize in advance for any unintentional omission or neglect and will be pleased to insert the appropriate acknowledgement to companies or individuals in any subsequent edition of this book.

'With the coming of Krupa, it was slam, bam, alacazan, with the rim shots exploding like roman candles in the skies of the mid-Thirties.'

George Frazier

'Gene was as magnetic as a movie star . . .'

Anita O'Day

'. . . he was the first jazz musician to become a matinee idol.'

Whitney Balliett

'I was grunting and sweating as if I was in a steel mill.'

Gene Krupa

'Krupa had a habit of accompanying his drumming with a somewhat repellent brand of showmanship . . .'

Charles Wilford

'Gene Krupa had a seventy-two inch heart'

Eddie Condon

'He was class.'

Benny Goodman

INTRODUCTION

Wednesday, 27 June 1973: four men are gathered in the CBS studio at 49 East 52nd Street in New York City. Two are white, two black, all are in their sixties, greying, prosperous-looking. They could be anything an onlooker wants them to be: bankers, real estate agents, doctors, lawyers. In fact, they are four men who, long ago in the 1930s, created a storm of enthusiasm in show business equalled only by Frank Sinatra in the 1940s and Elvis Presley and the Beatles in the 1960s. Collectively, they are the Benny Goodman Quartet. Individually, they are known familiarly to fans across the world—who perhaps have never come any closer than a gramophone record—as Benny, Teddy, Lionel and Gene.

Benny Goodman, thin and bespectacled in his twenties and only a little heavier in his sixties, plays clarinet; Teddy Wilson, as reserved and elegant in appearance as in performance, is at the piano; Lionel Hampton, forever bubbling with extrovert enthusiasm, is a multi-instrumentalist but in this context plays only the vibraphone. The final member of the Quartet is the drummer. In his sixties he is small and broad-shouldered and has greying hair where forty years before he had been slim and raven-haired with film star good looks. He is Gene Krupa, a man whose wholehearted approach to his music completely changed the role of the drummer in jazz.

The four men are in the CBS studio for a rehearsal the day before a New York concert appearance which is already sold out. They do not need the rehearsal in order to decide what to do and how to do it. Over the years, as Benny observes when they are through, 'We did an awful lot of playing together. It never left us. Even so, you worry. You wonder if you're going to get off the ground. I thought we got off the ground today, way off.' The real reason for the rehearsal is to ensure that Gene

Krupa can manage a complete performance. Clearly a sick man, he remarks to journalist Tom Buckley, who is present, that he wants to be sure that he can 'hack it'.

'This is the first time I've tried to play since I got out of the hospital,' he explains, adding optimistically, 'They say I've got a benign form of leukaemia. It can be controlled, but I've got to get a transfusion every couple of weeks and I've got to take it kind of easy.'

*   *   *   *

The following day, the Benny Goodman Quartet performed at the concert to the great satisfaction of the audience. Gene did take it kind of easy, ending the Quartet's set with a performance of *Sing, Sing, Sing* that was but a shadow of his former show-stopping performances on this old flagwaver. The fans didn't mind. If there was anything lacking on-stage they could provide the missing ingredients from forty-year-long memories.

This show was the latest in a string of reunion concerts given by the group since the early 1960s and their popularity showed no more signs of dimming than did their individual enthusiasm. It seemed as if they could go on forever but, of course, they couldn't.

There were a couple more appearances during the next few weeks and another on 18 August at Saratoga Springs. Two months after that, on 16 October 1973, Gene Krupa died.

Musicians who change jazz are inspired innovators: Louis Armstrong, Charlie Parker and their like. Gene Krupa was never an innovative genius, yet apart from changing beyond recognition the role of the jazz drummer he also provided the inspiration for his own and succeeding generations of drummers. With his handsome, overwrought, gesticulating presence both on-stage and on-screen, he provided a lasting visual image of the Swing Era. His wild performing persona, allied to a sensationalized phony drugs-bust in California in the 1940s, forged a lasting impression of the jazz drummer as junkie. It was then, and remains, an unfortunate and wholly inaccurate image because Gene Krupa was a dedicated, hard-working musician and a kindly, religious man. It is also unfair that he should be blamed for the tiresome idolization of drummers which came in his wake. He deserves a better memorial than that.

Most artists, be they painters, writers, or musicians, are products of their times. They are influenced by background, by circumstances often far beyond the sometimes narrow compass of their lives, by their predecessors, and their peers. Gene Krupa was no exception to this. His playing style, his music, his personality, his behaviour on-stage and off, were all shaped by the times through which he lived. To understand him and his musical style it is necessary to know the background of those times; the places where he lived and worked; the musicians he learned from and with whom he played. In exploring that background it will be possible also to determine the measure of a man who, in his turn, helped forge such a lasting impression of his era.

To have achieved the massive international acclaim, which was Gene's in his heyday, is all the more remarkable when his origins are considered. As the youngest son of a large family of Polish immigrant stock, born in 1909 on Chicago's tough South Side, he could very easily have fallen into crime or disappeared into the city's factories and mills like so many working class kids of his generation. But he had a burning ambition to be a musician and nothing was allowed to stand in his way.

In fulfilling that ambition he was aided by a fortuitous sense of timing. For anyone wanting to be a jazz musician there was no better place in which to grow up than Chicago in the 1920s.

CHAPTER 1

PRELUDE TO A STOMP
CHICAGO AND ALL THAT JAZZ

'Having seen it, I urgently desire never to see it again. It is inhabited by savages.'

Rudyard Kipling

Gene Krupa was born on 15 January 1909, the last child of Bartley and Ann to grow to adulthood. His parents were both children of Polish immigrants. Catholics, the Krupas had a large family; there were two girls and six boys ahead of Gene who was twenty-three years younger than the Krupas' first-born. As he remarked to jazz writer and critic Rudi Blesh, they 'originated the generation gap'. (Pianist-singer Bobby Scott, who worked with Gene in the 1950s and knew him better than most, has written that Gene once spoke of a younger brother whose tragic disappearance in suspicious circumstances deeply saddened the family.)

With most of his siblings working and earning much-needed money for the family, Gene was indulged by his mother, who wanted one of her seven sons to follow tradition and enter the church. Gene was the first for whom this was a realistic option.

His early schooling took place locally, at St Bridget's, followed by the Immaculate Conception school on the far South Side. He was, however, encouraged to earn his keep and was soon gaining work experience at the music store where his older brother, Pete, worked. Gene, an alert, dark-eyed, black-haired, pleasant ten-year-old, was hired to carry out light cleaning duties, nothing too onerous or important. This was just as well for he spent most of his time at the store listening to records. This musical interest quickly developed and helped him keep his job because he soon had most titles and record numbers firmly memorized and could be called upon to supply much-needed information to the rest of the staff.

Chicago's 'Little Poland' in the early 1900s: the kind of scene which surrounded Gene as a child.

Life on the tough South Side was not easy for children. Crime was everywhere and it was easy to fall into bad ways. But the district also tended to make its inhabitants tough-minded. 'Guys were out having gang wars, hitting each other with rocks,' Gene later recalled, acknowledging the difficulty of finding time to practise music and, especially, of finding anyone with whom to play. 'Mostly it would have to be a girl to play the piano. Playing with a saxophone or something like that, my goodness, that was impossible. Where would you find a guy that played the saxophone?'

Yet, in later life, he always recalled his childhood with genuine affection. On the South Side—as in most American cities—kids, dressed in knickerbockers or jeans and, wearing pleated caps, would spend their evenings kicking goals between lamp posts or, when they were not fighting, sitting talking (and smoking cigarettes) on front steps.

In middle-age Gene developed a liking for the novels of James T. Farrell whose 'Studs Lonigan Trilogy' constantly evokes scenes in Chicago that closely resembled his own childhood experiences. In one such passage, which also demonstrates the racial antagonism that lies so close to the surface of American society, Studs returned to the area where he was born and walked along the sidewalk before stopping 'under the elevated structure just south of Fifty-ninth Street. A train rumbled overhead. Sometimes they'd played skinny, or had fights here. He moved on past a row of apartment buildings. In his time, they'd looked new and modern, with lawns and trimmed bushes in front of them. Now they seemed old. The niggers all over again, running down a neighbourhood. He heard a victrola record going:

> *I hate to see de evening sun go down,*
> *I hate to see de evening sun go down.*

'An elevated train blotted the song out momentarily, then he heard it again:

> *St Louis woman, wid her diamond rings . . .*

'He walked on. Niggers living in all these buildings, living their lives, jazzing, drinking, and having their kids, and flashing razors at each other.'

Although none of the other Krupas had demonstrated any significant musical ability, Gene showed an early flair and for a while played alto saxophone. But it was for the drums that he showed special interest and aptitude.

Like many other young children from homes where luxuries were few, when Gene was old enough to attend high school he took a spare-time job. In his case, he managed to combine need with pleasure by working as a soda-jerk at a dance hall on Wisconsin Beach, north of the city. He also played saxophone in the junior band which played there but contrived to try out the drum kit after the band had gone for the night and he soon developed a measure of skill. The absence of musical inclination among the family didn't stop Pete Krupa from buying his kid brother a set of drums and soon those basic skills were showing signs of development. Certainly they were enough to allow Gene to deputize for the regular drummer when he called in sick one night at the dance hall. The band was the The Frivolians, all of them youngsters like Gene. This was 1922 and he was thirteen years old—too young to enter the sometimes dubious world of jazz in Chicago.

In many respects, Chicago jazz reflected the city itself in the 1920s: earthy, rough-toned, bustling, energetic. More than most American cities, on its surface Chicago has always displayed healthy, brawling, qualities. Underneath, there are as many subtleties as can be found anywhere, but the city and its people wear their tough-guy image with pride. It is not surprising, then, that its music mirrors that toughness.

During the time when Gene Krupa was growing up, Chicago became for some the apparent, albeit temporary, centre of the jazz world. To become so, it needed to be a city of a certain character. The Chicago of the 1920s was surely that, but its go-ahead, anything-goes atmosphere was apparent a long time earlier.

From the start, Chicago's location left it little option but to grow and grow.

The city stands on a windswept area of land on the edge of the wide-open spaces of the mid-West. Positioned between the southwest corner of Lake Michigan, which connects to the Atlantic Ocean via navigable waterways, and a series of rivers linked to the Mississippi, which in turn flows into the Gulf of Mexico some 1,500 miles to the south, it is a perfect site for a trading post.

The Native Americans also knew the strategic value of the region and had a series of camps amidst the scrub oaks and pines that grew along the sandy lakeshore. From late in the seventeenth century and for the next hundred years, first the French, then the British, made life uncomfortable for the Native Americans who were unconvinced when the interlopers decided that the 'Red Indian' had no rights.

In 1803 a military post, Fort Dearborn, was built close to the mouth of the Chicago River on a site which had been occupied for the past few years by the man who became in legend, if not in fact, the first Chicagoan.

Jean Baptiste Pointe de Saible was a trader, well-educated, multi-lingual, originally from the Caribbean and of mixed parentage. His father appears to have been from a family of merchants in Quebec while his mother was reputedly a Negro slave. The fact that Chicago's first resident was non-white was the first in a long line of events which gave rise to the mistaken belief that the city which grew upon this spot was somehow favourable to blacks.

The restless and frequently urgent westward movement of new Americans, most of whom were flowing in ever-increasing numbers from the Old World, needed a jumping-off point before tackling the thousands of miles of plains and wilderness. The windy city of Chicago was ideally situated. Given its location between the otherwise unbroken series of waterways which connected the Great Lakes to the Gulf of Mexico, it was also well-placed to provide a trading centre for goods travelling along a north-south axis. After the opening of the Erie Canal and the expansion of the railroad systems, Chicago was also well-linked to the densely populated East Coast.

From the outset, the planners of this 'prairie seaport' had no doubt that Chicago would become a major city. It was laid out on the rectangular grid system, with 66ft wide streets and 16ft alleys. The new community thus looked good although the fact that beneath the surface was a deep layer of impermeable clay over limestone meant that there was no natural drainage. Consequently, during the winter months the wide streets became hazardous rivers of mud in which many unfortunate residents struggled and drowned.

After the Civil War the city's growth continued both in terms of population and in physical size but the fire of 1871 devastated a considerable number of the largely timber-built houses. Starting in a barn behind the O'Leary house on De Koven Street (in legend, as a result of Mrs O'Leary's cow kicking over a lantern), the fire destroyed an area two thirds of a mile wide by four miles in length. 100,000 were rendered homeless but, surprisingly, the official death toll was only 250 (although the number of transients in Chicago at any one time made a sure count impossible).

The fire sparked a new determination in Chicagoans. Within a week more than 5,000 temporary homes were built and hundreds of permanent structures were on their way. This time, timber was outlawed as a construction material. The mud-covered limestone beneath the city was used to manufacture cement and soon buildings of four, five and even eight storeys were springing up.

Many outlying townships were incorporated into Chicago and by 1890 the total population exceeded one million, ranking second only to New York. The World's Columbian Exposition of 1893, held in Jackson Park, attracted 21 million visitors who viewed in amazement what historian Edwin C. Rozwenc has called a 'dream city that was built along Chicago's lake front—a city of palaces and marble bridges arranged with great skill along the banks of magnificent lagoons—[and which] taught the vital lesson of the need of design and plan for whole cities'. Not that every visitor to Chicago liked it. The English writer Rudyard Kipling was far from impressed and didn't care who knew it.

Movement in the heart of the city was made easier by the introduction of cable cars which made a loop around the business section and in 1897 an elevated line, installed by the South Side Rapid Transit Company, improved upon earlier efforts and provided better access to residential areas. The South Side, hitherto the main, and already heavily congested, residential area was overtaken in popularity by the more remote North and West Sides—at least for those who could afford to move. Soon a new kind of shopping facility was offered to Chicagoans with the introduction of department stores. The best of these were set along State Street with pride of place going to Marshall Field's emporium.

The businesses upon which Chicago built itself were largely those of service and supply to the rest of the nation. McCormick made reapers, Pullman made railroad cars and freight wagons (and in 1894 was beleaguered by a strike which gained such proportions that President Cleveland sent in the army despite protests from State Governor Altgeld). Mostly, however, the city provided food, drawing in grain from the plains for storing and milling, livestock from south and west for slaughtering, processing and packing. Its proud boast that it was the 'hog capital of the world' was not idle, and poet Carl Sandburg ended one of his early Chicago poems:

'Laughing the stormy, husky, brawling, laughter of Youth,
  half-naked,
    sweating, proud to be Hog Butcher, Tool Maker,
  Stacker of Wheat,
    Player with Railroads and Freight Handler to the Nation.'

17

By 1910 over six million hogs and three million head of cattle came live into Chicago and left cured or canned to feed the population. The labour needed for this huge annual turnover was immense and was drawn largely from the swarms of European immigrants, with Poles and Lithuanians prominent.

The conditions in which these men, women and children worked were appalling but were conveniently overlooked until Upton Sinclair published his novel *The Jungle* in 1906. Although, unabashedly socialistic in its tone, the harrowing descriptions of working conditions in the stockyards caused a public outcry. In midsummer, Sinclair wrote: 'The dingy killing beds . . . became a very purgatory; one time, in a single day, three men fell dead from sunstroke. All day long the rivers of hot blood poured forth, until, with the sun beating down, and the air motionless, the stench was enough to knock a man over . . . The men who worked on the killing beds would come to reek with foulness, so that you could smell one of them fifty feet away . . . ' If the killing beds were bad, then the innermost regions of the processing plants, which made use of inedible parts of animals for fertilizer, were infinitely worse. There: 'In suffocating cellars where the daylight never came you might see men and women and children bending over whirling machines and sawing bits of bone . . . breathing their lungs full of fine dust, and doomed to die, every one of them, within a certain definite time.'

Not surprisingly, Sinclair's book aided the passing of the pure food laws and also did something, but not enough, for workers' conditions. Curiously, it did not, as might have been expected, turn America into a nation of vegetarians.

The origins of the population of Chicago at this time were as mixed as New York's. The great waves of immigrants from the Old World brought in millions every year but, despite the myth of America as the 'melting pot' of nations, most newcomers retained their old allegiances. Chicago and New York each had a 'Little Italy' and other communities wherein was spoken only Italian or Yiddish, Greek, German or Polish.

Like many other immigrant groups, the Poles had fled Europe a few steps ahead of hunger or oppressors or both. Predominantly Catholic, the Poles brought with them an idealistic vision of their heritage. If Poland (Polska) was where they were born then America was Poland in exile (Polonia). This was a place where they could recover their strength and unity and keep faith with the Polish nation while waiting for the restoration of the Polish state. Just as different nationalities kept to themselves, so they were subjected to ignorant prejudice by others. When one businessman was asked how many Poles were in town he thought his questioner was asking about the poles the electricity company was putting up. When the question was rephrased he was dismissive of the Polish people: 'Oh! I don't know; they're no good.'

For many Poles, among them the Krupa family, Chicago's West and South Sides became Poland in exile, but the dream was better than reality. According to figures produced in 1894, although congestion was worse in some parts of New York at the same time, it was three times worse in the Polish district on the West Side than in the slums of Tokyo and Calcutta.

Apart from immigrants from Europe there was another major influx of residents to Chicago, one which was to have a far-reaching effect upon the city's musical development.

For many years black Americans had looked upon Chicago as a very special place. In William M. Tuttle's phrase, 'To Southern blacks, Chicago was not only a city; it was a state of mind.' While, doubtless, most had never heard of Jean Baptiste Pointe de Saible, all were surely aware that Chicago was a major stopping place on the Underground Railroad along which escaped slaves had fled the cruelties and oppression of the Deep South. Although their ultimate destination was Canada, few made it across the border. Indeed, for many escaped slaves it was good going if they crossed even their own state boundaries, let alone the Mason-Dixon line. For those born on a plantation or in one of the tawdry communities which sprang up around the turpentine farms of the South, the sheer size of America was beyond comprehension.

Nevertheless, some did make it to Canada, and a reasonably large number stopped just a little short and made their home in Chicago. A decade before the Civil War there was a sizable black population in the city, but despite this they never succeeded in becoming fully integrated. Between the ending of the war and the end of the century the black population grew, but on all sides they were prevented from becoming a part of the mainstream of civic life. Fenced in by legal barriers, denied basic civil rights, they were chiefly restricted to working in service despite being resident in the nation's greatest industrial city.

At the time of Chicago's incorporation in 1837 there were fewer than 100 blacks in a population of more than 4,000; by 1910 the proportion remained about the same with 44,000 out of a total population which exceeded two million. This slow but steady influx of blacks continued through the early years of the twentieth century and was usually welcomed by the resident

19

black community. The white residents of Chicago were, of course, markedly less anti-black than anywhere in the South and the city was more open than most other urban centres in the North (New Orleans showed a fairly relaxed attitude during the same period). The outbreak of war in Europe cut off the supply of immigrant labour and hence upgraded the importance of blacks in the eyes of the factory owners. The attitude of the white population changed towards blacks, and for the worse.

The steady migration from the South became a flood. Most of the newcomers were regarded by the resident blacks of Chicago as crude and lacking in even the most basic of society's requirements—such as personal cleanliness. Chicago's leading black newspaper, the *Defender*, was similarly aware, urging its readers not to go onto the streets wearing old, dirty or ragged clothes. 'Go clean up north,' the paper pleaded, before going on to state, somewhat dubiously, that whereas 'In the south a premium was put upon filth and uncleanliness. In the north a badge of honour is put on the man or woman who is clean.'

The existing black community roundly criticized their brothers fearing, rightly as it turned out, that their presence would antagonize the whites who had, hitherto, tolerated the blacks within their midst even though they had never accepted them as fellow citizens. Discrimination and segregation became a matter of fact, assiduously pursued by middle-class blacks and most whites. In particular, the white working class feared that the newcomers would take away their jobs and overrun their homes.

The majority of the new black population headed for the South Side. Earlier, immigrant families from northern Europe had moved out ahead of a wave of eastern and southern Europeans; now those who could afford to move made way for the blacks, and by 1920, 90% of the black population of 110,000 lived on the South Side. The majority made their home in an area bounded by Twelfth and Thirty-ninth Streets and by State Street and the Lakeshore. Earlier, this had been a prestige district with fashionable residences along Prairie and Calumet Avenues. As blacks edged into these districts, the whites moved out to Kenwood and Hyde Park (which in 1909 saw the city's first serious outbreak of racial violence), to Woodlawn and Englewood. Hemmed in as they were, the black population faced tensions from without and fearful congestion within.

Housing conditions were appalling and so too was the general health of the South Side residents. Although Chicago's overall death rate could be compared favourably with other major cities worldwide, the death rate of blacks was twice that of whites.

20

State Street

State Street, Chicago. For a while it compared favourably with New York's Seventh Avenue as a main jazz artery.

Stillbirths and death from tuberculosis, syphilis, pneumonia and nephritis placed it on a par with Bombay.

Race relations in Chicago deteriorated rapidly during the period of greatest expansion in the black population, exacerbated as it was by competition for jobs. Labour relations were uneasy, with white union organizers paying little heed to those blacks who tried to join the union and who were actively antagonistic towards those providing scab labour even in the hated stockyards. The unions wanted blacks to add weight to their numbers, but they didn't want them as union brothers.

21

As William Tuttle has expressed it, racial superiority was 'nurtured on the killing floors in the stockyards, on all-white blocks threatened with black occupancy, and in parks and on beaches that were racially contested'.

In Chicago in 1919, a year which saw race riots around the world, trouble flared on a hot summer's day when a young black boy, swimming in Lake Michigan, strayed from the 25th Street beach and came within stone-throwing distance of white bathers on the 29th Street beach. The boy, Eugene Williams, was hit by a stone and despite the efforts of his companions he drowned. Within minutes of Eugene's death the first blows, and then shots, were exchanged and five days later, when the riot faded, it left about 40 dead and more than 500 injured.

Racial violence was not restricted to conflict between blacks and whites. In the early 1920s, as a new wave of immigrants came in from Mexico, the Poles along with the Italians were the leaders of a concerted and violent attempt to deter them.

Quite clearly, then, the general atmosphere was such that any child born into a Polish family in Chicago in 1909 could be expected to mature with in-built and immovable prejudices. That the most famous son of the Polish Krupas proved to be a leading figure in the integration of black and white musicians in jazz, at a time when it needed great strength of mind to even acknowledge blacks as social equals, is all the more remarkable.

In 1915 the black vote had helped elect Republican William Hale 'Big Bill' Thompson as mayor of Chicago. Having gained power, Big Bill was smart enough not to renege on campaign promises and he was soon regarded by blacks (somewhat shortsightedly) as another Lincoln. At the 1919 election the black vote was decisive in returning Big Bill to office. Part of his programme allowed almost free rein to hoodlums and racketeers whose growing empire included clubs and cabarets, gin mills and speakeasies. This was just one of several factors that made Chicago in the 1920s a main centre in America for the growth of popular entertainment in all its many forms. Especially significant in Chicago was 'lowbrow' music and in particular one form which had been growing in popularity since the turn of the century.

This was jazz, and it was against the improbable background of overpopulation, bad housing, poor health, racial tension and riots, questionable political practices, crime and public waywardness, that the music took root in Chicago. In the next decade it helped draw together, often in uneasy alliance and with much less integration than many would later allow, the black and white races.

Although New York remained the mecca for all branches of the entertainment industry in America, jazz included, Chicago now drew much attention. In part, this was due to some changes which took place in the music but mostly it was because of the infectious excitement of the Chicago jazz scene which took hold of the imagination and which, in passing, created more than its share of legends.

For young Gene Krupa the odds against his ever becoming a part of Chicago's jazz life appeared impossible. Despite the cooperation of his brother Pete, who had bought that first set of drums, the other young Krupas were not impressed that Gene was spending so much time playing music (playing around with music, they thought) that he failed his school examinations. They ganged up on Mrs Krupa. If they had to work to support the family, then so should he.

But Ann Krupa, apart from displaying an understandable feeling for her late-arriving son, was aware that Gene's enthusiasm was very real although quite clearly she had no idea—and neither had he—whether or not this youthful enthusiasm was backed with any real talent.

Therefore, Ann Krupa struck a bargain with her son. Still hopeful that he would enter the priesthood, she persuaded him to go to St Joseph's College, a preparatory seminary at Rensselaer, Indiana, just across the state line. His tuition and board (the college was fifty miles from home) would add to the the family's financial problems because about this time Gene's father died, but Ann Krupa overcame protests. The other side of the bargain with his mother was that if, after a reasonable period there, Gene still wanted to play music she wouldn't stand in his way.

At St Joseph's Gene played baseball, another childhood passion, but also found an opportunity to further his musical interests thanks to the presence at the college of Father Ildefonse Rapp, the professor of music who, unlike many others of his generation, was not automatically opposed to jazz.

After a year at St Joseph's, Gene decided he had had enough and returned home. This was not through any lack of faith in his religion—far from it, in fact, for his devotion to God and the Church remained important to him for the rest of his life. But, strong as his religious commitment was, it gave way before his musical ambitions. Ann Krupa gave in and thereafter backed him wholeheartedly in his attempt to fulfil his ambition to become a professional musician. Given the prevailing attitude of most white Americans, it is not surprising that, if he wasn't to enter the church, she would have preferred him to have been interested in something, anything, other than jazz.

Jazz was not for 'decent' people. Jazz was the music of the lowlife, the whorehouse, the sleazy bar. All groups in American society condemned the jazz world. The black newspaper *The Chicago Messenger* criticized it heartily, thus laying, in some small measure at least, the perpetuated myth that all blacks liked jazz. But jazz was gaining acceptance, due in part to the fact that American society was changing, and especially its popular culture.

1919 had seen the publication of the first successful tabloid newspaper, the New York *Daily News*; motor cars, mostly open-topped, were becoming more readily available, allowing ordinary people, if not the poor, to get about and seek entertainment. Movies were providing some of that entertainment and making fortunes for the darlings of the day: Charlie Chaplin, Mary Pickford, Douglas Fairbanks. A major revolution of popular culture took place late in 1920 when Station KDKA in East Pittsburgh began transmission. The radio station's fare was mostly gramophone records although live music was tried but abandoned due to acoustic problems. The station then tried broadcasting a band out of doors but in a tent. The tent blew away, so the entire operation, tent and all, was transferred indoors. The result was so successful that the indoor tent was replaced with hanging drapes for acoustic effect and thus paved the way for the modern recording and broadcasting studio. Radio was in, and when tens of thousands heard live commentary on Jack Dempsey's 4th Round knockout of Georges Carpentier, everyone wanted to own a set. Radio sales in 1922 were a massive $60 million but by 1929 they had rocketed to a staggering $842 million.

Many of those millions of Americans who couldn't afford the new-fangled automobile, and hence could not get out for entertainment, could raise the money for the equally new-fangled but much cheaper radio. The nation stayed home in droves, listening to their favourite shows and lost what passing interest they had shown in world affairs. The failure of Woodrow Wilson to establish a meaningful League of Nations coincided with the fading of threats of communist subversion. As Frederick L. Allen observed, 'How could one bother about the Red Menace if one was facing such momentous questions as how to construct a loop aerial?'

There was much more, of course, than merely listening to the radio, especially in Chicago. Ever since the turn of the century, the city was host to an impressive array of writers which led H. L. Mencken to describe it as the nation's literary capital. The names included Theodore Dreiser, Sherwood Anderson, Sandburg, Frank Norris, Sinclair and Farrell and, later, Richard Wright and Nelson Algren. Such writers and their fellow artists and architects reshaped the city, and effected changes which helped alter American society beyond recognition.

However, far from the least of the factors which changed society was something neither literary nor artistic. This was the Eighteenth Amendment to the Constitution of the United States which, in 1919, prohibited the sale and transportation of liquor. Suddenly, men and women who liked a drink, be it whiskey, gin or beer, were faced with becoming secretive drinkers or criminals or both. Of course, they could have given up drinking, which is what the legislators hoped, but for neither the first time nor the last, the nation's lawmakers gravely underestimated public needs.

In all major cities, night spots and bars opened their doors, however cautiously. In Chicago, too much caution wasn't needed as the booze-pedalling hoodlums exercised considerable powers of persuasion upon the city's police force. Prohibition or not, one statistical source suggests that in Chicago alone, an estimated (and barely credible) 12,000 such places were in existence in 1922 (and four years later had doubled their numbers). Given such proliferation, the laws against alcohol, and the city's reputation for being wide-open and wild, it is not at all surprising that Chicago became a haven for criminals and for the entertainers needed to perform in all the clubs.

The link between crime, prostitution (which had been legal in Chicago until 1912) and booze on the one hand and jazz on the other, already forged in New Orleans, was strengthened in Chicago both in reality and (even more so) in the public imagination.

Even if jazz had been played in brothels, that would have been the least of the places where it could be heard. There were countless nightspots in the city which provided entertainment of which live music was a staple. Not all of it was jazz, of course, but a substantial proportion was. Fortuitously, the dominant ethnic groups among the gangsters, the Italians and the Jews, showed a marked preference for this lively and energetic form of music.

In the early years before the rise of white jazzmen, whether Chicago-born or based or not, the important and best jazz came from black musicians. The impact of black jazzmen upon the white musicians of Chicago was profound. Early jazz had been heard in Chicago for several years. Such pre-jazz performers as ragtime pianist and singer Tony Jackson played there. The date of his visit is imprecise but was probably around the year of Gene Krupa's birth. Shortly after Jackson came pianist-composer-singer and raconteur Jelly Roll Morton. The arrival of the Original Creole Band in 1913 began to influence musical tastes and, significantly, they played extended engagements in the heart of the South Side's Black Belt. As Paul Eduard Miller's researches show, the Original Creole Band was followed by numerous other bands, black and white. The musicians who played there included such major talents as Manuel Perez, Lorenzo Tio, Nick LaRocca and Sidney Bechet (who was heard by Will Marion Cook and hired for a trip to Europe in 1919 where his astonishing technique startled audiences and musicians of all kinds). Many of the visiting bands originated in New Orleans, thus laying the ground for the simplistic myth of jazz: that it was born in New Orleans and travelled upriver to Chicago before moving southwest to Kansas City and east to New York. In reality jazz was everywhere and spreading multi-directionally, but certainly New Orleans was a major centre during its formative years, and equally beyond dispute is the fact that Chicago was where a great expansion of public attention took place in the 1920s.

The district known as the Loop, named for the early cable car circuit, became the centre of Chicago's theatrical life, and many theatregoers would round out their evening's entertainment by taking a short journey on the new elevated railroad to the heart of the Black Belt. Short as that El-ride was, it transported them to another world.

Within the Black Belt were countless clubs and cabarets and bars and most visiting bands and musicians homed in on it. In some parts of the district the places where music could be heard stood shoulder to shoulder. Two such areas, the corners of Thirty-first and State Street and of Thirty-fifth and State became known as the 'Section'. Soon, State Street was a musical equivalent to New York's Seventh Avenue.

The movement of musicians towards Chicago was not an event that was separate from the massive migration of blacks towards northern industrial centres in search of work. Musicians followed naturally, aware that if their brothers found work they would have money to spend on entertainment. And, of course, the musicians were not just jazzmen. Blues singers from all parts of the nation began a drift towards Chicago which soon became (and remains) a major centre for the blues.

As indicated, the growth of Chicago as America's second largest city was as attractive to white musicians as it was to blacks. In 1914 a band arrived which featured Nick LaRocca and was a forerunner of the Original Dixieland Jazz Band. What they found there somewhat surprised them. As recounted by Paul Eduard Miller and George Hoefer, the band was hired to play at the grandly named Casino Gardens. The band's drummer, Anton Lada, remarked of this venue: 'I thought we had dives in New Orleans, but for low-down barrel-house, the Casino had anything in New Orleans beat to shreds.'

Over the next few years bands and musicians, black and white but mostly black, came into Chicago sometimes on tour, often to stay. In 1918, with the migration in full spate, an important job became available at the Royal Garden (later to become the Lincoln Garden) which was located on Thirty-first Street, seven blocks from State Street. A band was formed which had in its ranks such outstanding New Orleanians as drummer Paul Barbarin and clarinetist Johnny Dodds. The man building up the band, bass-player Bill Johnson, needed a top-flight cornet player and sent to New Orleans for the man who was currently the best in the business, Joe Oliver.

Zutty Singleton, one of the New Orleans-born drummers from whom Gene learned in his early years in jazz.

The band that King Oliver led at the Lincoln Garden and which doubled every night at the Dreamland on State Street, just around the corner from Thirty-fifth Street, became the matrix for every up and coming band and the source of much professional envy from established musicians. In 1922, after touring the West Coast, Oliver returned to Chicago with a band which now comprised Johnny Dodds on clarinet; Honore Dutrey, trombone; Ed Garland, bass; Lil Hardin, piano; Baby Dodds on drums; and if that wasn't enough to scare the opposition, he proceeded to bring up to Chicago another New Orleans cornet player to share his front line duties. The newcomer was Louis Armstrong. Every member of King Oliver's band was now equipped to provide an object lesson for would-be jazzmen, black and white, in Chicago. Most significant of these was, of course, Armstrong but for the moment his star was slightly overshadowed by that of his mentor, King Joe.

Before they could be taken seriously, the young white Chicago jazz musicians had much prejudice to overcome. Not only was there racial animosity, now widespread despite the surface impression of Chicago as a place where blacks were welcome, but there was also intense disapproval from their parents at their interest in the music played by the black jazzmen. For this older generation popular music meant such songs as *Meet Me Tonight in Dreamland* (which did *not* refer to the Dreamland Cafe), *Put On Your Old Grey Bonnet, Casey Jones, Ciribiribin, My Wife's Gone to the Country* and (surprisingly for a nation which, largely, had never even heard of the Isle of Man) a slightly reworded version of *Has Anybody Here Seen Kelly?*, all of which were first published in America in 1909, the year of Gene Krupa's birth.

The dance halls were tough places, even for the musicians. Gene recalled playing a job at Wagner's Hall where every night fights would break out among the paying customers. When the dance ended and the band was packing to go home, the fight would be still going on, dangerously close to the musicians. Fortunately, Gene had become something of a favourite with the crowd. 'I'd move my drums to the edge of the stage, so I could get them off. And some cat, some real mean guy who was one of the gang leaders, would give a shrill whistle and they'd stop and clear a path for me [then] start swinging again as soon as I left.'

With musicians obliged to frequent such tough venues, the jazz life was inevitably regarded with considerable disdain by society at large but the young Chicagoans were not to be put off.

To be a Chicagoan in jazz parlance it was not necessary to

*Jimmy McPartland,
one of Gene's earliest
musical collaborators,
here joining forces
with Gene's 1940s
superswinging singer,
Anita O'Day.*

have been born there, or even to have spent any time in the city. Rather, it needed a musician to be imbued with a certain spirit and to possess certain attitudes of mind. Consequently, the converse also applied; some jazzmen who were born and raised and began their careers in Chicago did not qualify as Chicagoans. Thus, Wingy Manone, from New Orleans, was a Chicagoan, so too was Volly de Faut who came from Arkansas, and Rod Cless and Bix Beiderbecke from Iowa (although Bix soon moved on to more exalted status), and Jess Stacy from Missouri or Pee Wee Russell from Oklahoma. Benny Goodman, who was born and raised in Chicago, was not a Chicagoan in the sense in which the main group of practitioners thought of themselves.

This group was fluid and ever-changing but the hard core were Jimmy McPartland, cornet; Floyd O'Brien, trombone; Frank Teschemacher, clarinet and alto saxophone; Bud Freeman, tenor saxophone; Dave North, piano; Dick

McPartland, banjo; Jim Lannigan, bass; and Dave Tough, drums. Of these, Lannigan (born 1902), was the oldest, and Tough (born 1908) the youngest. Several of this group were still at school: Austin High, near Washington Boulevard and Central Avenue. Collectively, they became known as the Austin High School Gang.

They modelled themselves upon the New Orleans Rhythm Kings, a band that had grown out of the Friar's Society Orchestra and which played at Chicago's Friar's Inn. As Jimmy McPartland observed (in *Hear Me Talkin' to Ya*, the taped reminiscences of jazzmen gathered from many sources and edited for publication by Shapiro and Hentoff), 'We were too young to get into Friar's Inn, so the only way we could hear the Rhythm Kings was to go down and stand in the doorway and listen. It was great when someone opened the door and we could hear it louder.'

The young would-be musicians formed a semi-pro band, called themselves The Blue Friars, and were soon a force, albeit a minor one, to be reckoned with in and around the Windy City.

Drummer Dave Tough was the thinker of the group, and it was he who was forever analyzing and seeking to improve their music and their understanding of what they and their idols were doing. It was in this intellectualizing of their music that the Chicagoans moved furthest from other jazzmen (although they were a long way short of what was to happen in jazz many years later). Not that they allowed the intellectualization to get out of hand. Even if, to them, the correct classically-based training Benny Goodman underwent in his search for perfection was anathema, they did not take themselves so seriously that they didn't enjoy their life and music. Dave Tough might indulge in poetry and jazz readings but the 'wild West Side mob' (yet another of the numerous tags hung upon them) liked a different kind of good time. Interestingly, the black New Orleanians rated Benny Goodman far more highly than did his fellow citizens of Chicago. For the most part, the New Orleans jazzmen, although often dismissed as primitive musicians, were highly skilled and practised performers who aspired to and often attained a high level of musical skill, and admired such qualities in others.

But the young Chicagoans wanted something other than what Benny offered. Stylistically, the Chicagoans preferred a fiery urgency in their music, giving it qualities which reflected the spirit of the city.

Perhaps the best, non-technical and most succinct description of the Chicago style comes from George Avakian's sleeve notes for the Columbia album, 'Chicago Style in Jazz': 'The tension, urgency and fire of Chicago Style are external as well as internal matters. An "explosion" at the end of every chorus sends the succeeding one off to a catapult start; those two-bar flares are played by everyone, even in choruses which are otherwise solos. Stop-and-go devices, shifting rhythmic patterns (including a kind of double-time known as the "Chicago shuffle"), varying dynamics and all-out finishes capped by "double endings" (the addition of two extra bars to the last chorus) are used to create a supercharged atmosphere. The ensemble holes are filled like Nature tackling a vacuum; the solos are almost agonized. Phrases are short, jagged, almost spit out. There is a Chicago tone, too—tart, slightly off-pitch, with a buzzy, rough edge. Strong notes stop mattering; driving, on-the-beat excitement is what counts.'

Apart from their musical differences, the Chicagoans also began to develop social traits which were far removed from Benny Goodman's scholarly attitude. It was the arrival in their midst of Eddie Condon which saw to it that for succeeding generations of jazz musicians and fans, a serious capacity for hard liquor was required for anyone claiming to be a genuine Chicagoan.

Condon and his 'barefoot mob' were soon to be found working wherever anyone was prepared to hire them. The group formed various bands sometimes clearly separate but often with shifting, frequently interchangeable personnel. There was the McPartland-Freeman band, McPartland-Russell, Eddie Condon's, and the Summa Cum Laude band. Yet, for all their titles, the music retained the growingly recognizable Chicago style.

Working wherever they could, the Austin High Gang improved steadily. (Eddie Condon never fully approved of that particular tag. Many years later, driving down a West Chicago street with Jim Lannigan he noticed a large school and asked what it was. 'Lannigan replied that it was Austin High School. Krupa, Sullivan and I were supposed to be part of the Austin High Gang, a name pinned on us by critics who have to put labels on everything. I couldn't spell Austin High. I'm glad I finally saw it.') The growing popularity of movie theatres gave the group additional opportunities for work although, as Condon has recounted in his autobiographical works, their enthusiasm for jazz led them to overlook their real purpose in being there in the first place. Playing in the pit at the Commercial Theatre on the far South Side, a movie house which catered to the Mexican community, Eddie recalled how they 'were supposed to watch the news-reel and play appropriate accompaniment; we seldom did. One night in the middle of *Clarinet Marmalade* I looked up and saw a French general placing a wreath on the Tomb of the Unknown Soldier. Just then Dave Tough went into an explosion on the drums. Things like that confused the Mexicans.'

It wouldn't have confused one member of the audience because Gene Krupa, a few years younger than the Condon mob, had discovered the band and was seeing as many shows as he could.

During 1926 and 1927 Gene, now a good-looking but still diminutive teenager, worked extensively in one band after another. Few of his engagements were in genuine jazz bands. Mostly, he worked dance dates but the experience proved invaluable in allowing him to develop his technique even if it restricted the style in which he wanted to play. He worked with the Seattle Harmony Kings, the Hoosier Bell Hops, Leo Shukin, and Joe Kayser who was one of the best known dance band leaders of the region. He also worked with Thelma Terry's Playmates. Thelma, a bass player, was one of the few female bandleaders around Chicago at the time. Her Playmates were otherwise an all-male outfit. Gene also worked in the 'Benson Orchestra'. This was a band (or, often, bands) put together by the Benson Booking Agency for gigs in and around Chicago.

Despite the enthusiasm of the Austin High Gang, the leading Chicagoan band was the Wolverines which featured Bix Beiderbecke and when he moved to New York various personnel changes took place. Jimmy McPartland replaced Bix and soon began bringing in his old pals. When Dave Tough decided to join the Wolverines, he went in search of Gene and asked him if he would like to take his place in the Blue Friars. 'Would I!' Gene said, and became a regular with the band. But, unlike some of the others he couldn't afford to play for nothing or to sit around waiting for jazz-only gigs and kept up his connection with the Benson office. Indeed, there were occasions when he was able to get work for those of the gang who were readers and not so dead set against commercialism that they wouldn't play anything but jazz.

Even with the commercial dates, this was the time when Gene began to develop as a jazz drummer of considerable capability. He achieved this partly through playing, partly through listening. Fortunately, most of the time, he played with and listened to the right kind of music and musicians.

CHAPTER 2

PAYIN' THEM DUES BLUES
SCUFFLING AND STARVING

'I think we've got something.'   Tommy Rockwell

Like it or not (and many decidedly did not), the breezy, biting music of the Chicagoans echoed not only the weather which Chicago endured but also the tough, gutsy, uncomprising attitude of the city's residents at large.

The new style, sought by the Austin High School Gang and their growing band of admirers and emulators, concerned itself with music for its own sake. They were brashly confident that they were right (as are all younger generations who set about changing the old order). As Richard Hadlock comments, 'The Chicagoans were, by and large, a cocky and self-important group. [Frank] Teschemacher was moody and serious, [Jimmy] McPartland brash and outgoing, [Dave] Tough cynical and questioning, [Bud] Freeman impulsive and ingenuous, but all were convinced that they had something no one else had, and each member of the gang bristled with enthusiasm.'

Believing their distillation of the essence of New Orleans music to be purer than that being currently offered by the transplanted New Orleanians themselves, they set about reshaping the role of each member of the band and high on the list came the drummer.

The task of filling that aural vacuum, referred to by George Avakian, fell to the drummer. He filled it with sound and, being capable of more sheer volume than anyone else, the drummer's capacity to make or break a band became critical. Additionally, of course, it was still the drummer's job to help provide the beat and few were capable of doing this as well as becoming stylistic innovators.

King-pin of them all was Dave Tough. Richard Hadlock credits Dave with creating those two major facets of Chicago style, the explosion and shuffle rhythm. As indicated, the explosion is that 'sudden flare preceding each repetition of the initial melodic statement [which occurs] in a conventional song structure. . .' while shuffle rhythm is 'a staccato, heavily accented eighth-note pattern usually applied to the bridge, or a release, of a song.'

Dave has also been credited with urging his fellow gang members to open their ears, if selectively, to the music that was all around them. For the principal drummers among the Chicagoans (Dave himself, George Wettling and Gene Krupa) there was certainly plenty to hear and learn from.

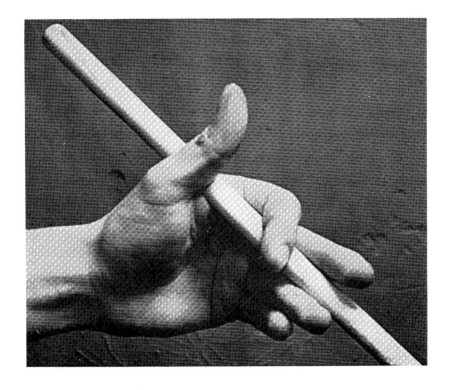

The hand that launched a thousand drum rolls.

Just who it was that encouraged Gene to go hear the New Orleans master drummers Baby Dodds, Tubby Hall and Zutty Singleton is open to some speculation. Dave Tough undoubtedly was one; Eddie Condon also clearly had a hand. And then there was Mezz Mezzrow.

Fortunately, the jazz world has never been short of 'characters' and Mezz certainly was one of them. Born in Chicago in 1900, Milton Mesirow, later Mezz Mezzrow, was an undistinguished (and occasionally quite dreadful) clarinet player but was completely immersed in the jazz spirit. Totally committed to the music, he was so convinced that only black

34

musicians could really play it that for many years he adopted black attitudes, speech patterns, personal and musical traits and even, almost forty years before the Civil Rights movement, deliberately 'passed' for black. Voluble and opinionated, Mezz had a belief in himself which matched that of Jelly Roll Morton's self-importance (but was nowhere nearly as justified). Mezzrow's autobiography, although liberally scattered with examples of his opinions of himself, paints a vivid picture of the jazz life. Replete with racy dialogue and gaudy anecdotes, it adds colour to the historical facts (which are largely absent in his writing). Reading between the lines it does become apparent that Mezzrow's undoubted popularity with some jazzmen stemmed more from his ability to provide endless quantities of (usually high-grade) marijuana than from any musical contribution he might make. For all its countless faults, it is a book which should be read by anyone interested in the atmosphere of the jazz life. Unfortunately, many who have read it also believe it all.

Mezzrow's account (first published in 1946) of how he alone helped shape Gene Krupa's drumming style makes fascinating reading; all the more so when set alongside Gene's own recollections reported by Leonard Feather (and published in 1957).

After stating that it was actually he who first heard about Gene, tracked him down, and introduced this 'neat, well-dressed, very good-looking youngster' to the Austin High Gang, Mezzrow goes on to declare that with Dave Tough on his way to play in France, he felt able to pass on to Gene all Dave's jazz drumming secrets.

'One important thing we worked out,' Mezz writes, 'was the difference between starting a roll or a sequence of beats with the left hand or the right hand, how the tone and inflection changed entirely when you shifted hands.'

Gene, according to Leonard Feather, states, 'I picked up from Zutty Singleton and Baby Dodds the difference between starting a roll or sequence of beats with the left or right hand and how the tone and inflection changed entirely when you shifted hands.'

Mezz: 'Then we went to work on the tom-toms, trying to get them in tune and studying the right times to use them; we kept punching holes in them with an ice-pick until they were pitched just right.'

Gene: 'Taking my cue from what I heard, I next went to work on the tom-toms trying to get them in tune and knowing when to use 'em. I punched holes in them with an ice-pick.'

Mezz: 'Next, remembering more of the things I'd learned from Zutty and Baby Dodds, I showed Gene how to keep the bass and the snare drum in tune, and to get cymbals that rung in tune and were pitched in certain keys. After that we got to the cowbell and the woodblock, messing with them until we got them pitched in tune with the right keys.'

Gene: 'Another trick I got from Baby Dodds was how to keep the bass and the snare drum in tune and how to get cymbals that rang in tune and were pitched in certain keys. Then came the cowbell and the woodblock.'

The passage of time had clearly affected someone's memory.

One of Mezzrow's pronouncements in this same passage of his book does contain a clear indication of the changing role of the drummer in jazz. 'I'd show [Gene] the secret that Dave Tough had dug, that there was a tonal pattern of harmony to be followed and that what seemed like a steady beat was really a sequence of different sounds accented at the right intervals, with just the correct amount of vibrations coming from the snare and the bass [drum] so that the other musicians who were improvising got the foundation to carry on and be more inventive.'

Gene had, by this time, undergone some formal tuition (from, among others, Roy C. Knapp whom he met at the Capitol Theatre on South Halstead Street in 1925), and was a rapidly improving musician. If he lacked the fluidity of Dave Tough (which would later allow Dave to make the Benny Goodman band sound so very different from how it did when Gene was its drummer), and the workmanlike solidity of George Wettling (who hailed from Wichita and was the Chicagoans second favourite drummer), he brought unbridled enthusiasm to his performance. Despite ranking third in this small hierarchy, in most respects he was, at this time, the most appropriate drummer for the exuberant Chicago-style jazz. ·

Most importantly, regardless of who was the prime-mover, he was certainly listening to everyone and everything. His reaction on first hearing Dave Tough was openly enthusiastic. 'I said, "Wow, Man." He said, "Hell, this ain't nothing. Let me take you to hear Baby Dodds." '

And Gene certainly did hear Baby, and Zutty, and Ollie Powell (who was with Jimmy Noone's band), and Tubby Hall. For all of them he professed reverent admiration. They were, in his phrase, 'something else'. And, from all of them, he learned eagerly.

Everything he heard was new and exciting, and revolutionized his own approach. 'Any idea that I knew

Dave Tough, the thinking Chicagoan's drummer.

anything about the skins had to go out the window once I started visiting those South Side joints.'

The attitude of Gene's mother to his frequenting such places was indicated by Mezz Mezzrow. One time, heading for a late night out on the town, Mezz asked Gene what his mother thought about it all. 'He said, "Oh, it'll be all right, Milton, as long as I'm with you. Momma thinks you're a genius and anything I do with you is OK." ' The fact that up to this point Ann Krupa had never met Mezz, having spoken to him only on the telephone, accounts for the absence of her customary good judgement.

Gene continued playing at every opportunity. Despite being unable to read music, he had earlier joined the American Musicians Union, which necessitated taking a test. 'The guy said, "Make a roll. That's it. Give us 50 bucks. You're in." ' Union membership had allowed him to play dance dates with the mickey-mouse bands the other Chicagoans so despised (and was a step towards the rather more selective American Federation of Musicians). Now, however, he was becoming more and more involved in the thriving jazz scene.

The sheer volume of clubs, cabarets and bars in the Section alone was enough to keep fans and musicians in ecstasies. Covering a distance of less than a mile on State Street there were the Elite, Dreamland, the Pekin, Panama, the Rose Garden, Blatz Beer Gardens, the Vendome and Lincoln Theatres, the Oriental Cafe, the Open Air Gardens, the Edelweiss, the Fiume Cafe, and many more besides. Louis Armstrong recalled: 'Things were jumping so around Chicago at that time, there was more work than a cat could shake a stick at. I was doubling from the Dreamland for a while. Then I stayed at the Vendome for only a year before I decided to double again.'

For visitors with any musical interest, a trip along State Street was a must. In later years, Gene Krupa recalled a night when the French composer Maurice Ravel visited the Sunset Cafe at 35th and Calumet and marvelled at 'Jimmy Noone's transcendent clarinet'.

All of the clubs had some connection with the underworld, even if only for the supply of bootleg booze or the payment of protection. Many were owned outright by gangsters who, naturally enough, frequented them. Such clientele could lead to unnerving moments for the musicians. Eddie Condon recalled the burly manager of one club who made Dave Tough solve his crossword puzzles for him. Jake, the manager, weighed close to three hundred pounds while Dave, a diminutive individual, barely tipped the scale at one third of that. One night Dave was so busy finishing Jake's puzzle that he was late for a set. As he hurried to the bandstand one customer didn't move. 'Dave put both hands against the man's shoulders. "Get the hell out of my way!" he said. One of the boys on the bandstand looked at Dave with admiration as he sat down at the drums. "I guess you don't care how long you live," he said. "Or aren't you afraid of Bottles Capone?" Bottles was Al's kid brother. Dave played the set involuntarily; he shook enough to beat the drums in perfect time. But Jake saved him; he couldn't afford to have his crossword puzzle expert damaged.'

Less fortunate were boogie-woogie pianist Clarence 'Pinetop' Smith who was shot to death while playing at a masonic hall on the West Side, and comedian Joe E. Lewis whose vocal cords were severed as a 'lesson' for daring to move to another club without permission from his gangster boss. (In 1957 Lewis was portrayed by Frank Sinatra in the movie *The Joker Is Wild*.) A not untypical night-club occurrence was gunplay, succinctly described by drummer George Wettling: 'We would see those rods come up—and duck. At the Triangle Club the boss was shot in the stomach one night, but we kept working. After that he walked sort of bent over.'

Of all the clubs, perhaps the most atmospheric, and certainly a musicians' favourite, was the Three Deuces at 222 North State Street. Benny Goodman's recollection fully evokes its atmosphere. 'The room downstairs, where [the musicians] jammed, was a dismal, unpainted place, with wooden walls, and no covering on the floor. Over on one side was an old beat-up piano. Sometimes when you'd go in there sober it almost knocked you off your feet. If the boys were going good, you'd be just as apt as not see the other fellows beating the rhythm on the wall with their hands when somebody took a chorus.'

Many of the clubs, the Three Deuces included, were pokey, windowless basement speakeasies and were very much 'men only' establishments. In the jargon of the day they were known as a 'blind pigs'. Daylight never filtered into such places and, in the expressive phrase of one-time jazz pianist turned entertainer, Jimmy Durante (who owned a night club in New York), the 'only fresh air to be had was what the customers brought in on their clothes'.

Unappetizing as it might sound, for musicians the Three Deuces seemed like heaven. There, they could play whatever they liked, and they liked to play jazz. The club attracted the great and the soon-to-be great. One night, when the Paul Whiteman band was in town playing the Chicago Theatre, Bix

38

Beiderbecke and Tommy Dorsey dropped in to jam with Eddie Condon, Frank Teschemacher, Glenn Miller, Benny Goodman and Gene Krupa. Later, Benny remarked of this occasion to jazz writer Arnold Shaw that Gene 'was beginning to play good drums'.

Among the gigs Gene played were at least two with his would-be mentor, Mezz Mezzrow. One engagement was at the Rendezvous in downtown Chicago where fellow band members included trombonist Floyd O'Brien and pianist Joe Sullivan. The other was a member of Mezz Mezzrow's Purple Grackle Orchestra. This was not descriptive of a Chicagoan-style hangover but came from the name of a club thirty miles out of Chicago on the road to Joliet (which housed the prison many Chicago club owners avoided with alarming ease). Mezzrow describes the establishment as 'beautiful modernistic Spanish-patio kind of roadhouse, lousy with heavy purple plush drapes all over the joint'. As to the origin of the club's name, Mezzrow admitted at the time of writing his book that he still didn't 'know what in hell a purple or any other colour grackle is'.

A much more important, and significant, gig came along on 9 December 1927. Red McKenzie was in town and trading insults with Eddie Condon who understandably failed to take seriously a musician who earned such a good living playing a comb and paper that he was quickly able to afford his very own kazoo. McKenzie listened to a band Eddie hastily gathered together to prove a few of his points about the Chicagoans' superior musical qualities. Impressed in spite of himself, McKenzie promised to persuade Tommy Rockwell of OKeh records to record the band. He succeeded and earned sufficient gratitude from Eddie to have a share of the band's name. The McKenzie-Condon Chicagoans comprised Jimmy McPartland on cornet; Frank Teschemacher, clarinet; Bud Freeman, tenor saxophone; Joe Sullivan, piano; Eddie Condon, banjo; Jim Lannigan, bass; and Gene Krupa on drums.

When the band arrived at OKeh's Chicago studios at Washington and Wells, Rockwell was visibly disturbed at the sight of Gene's drums being hauled in by the drummer and Mezz Mezzrow (who was determined not to be left out of the act). As Condon recalls in his autobiography, the OKeh executive stared across to where Mezz was helping Gene set up his drums. ' "What are you going to do with those?" Rockwell asked. "Play them," Krupa said simply. Rockwell shook his head. "You'll ruin our equipment. All we've ever used on records are snare drums and cymbals." Krupa, who had been practising every day at home, looked crushed. "How about letting us try them?"

I asked. "The drums are the backbone of the band. They hold us up." ' Eventually, Rockwell agreed but was still worried that the vibration from the heavier drums, the tom-toms and the bass drum, would knock the needle off the wax. This problem was overcome, as McPartland recalled, 'by laying down rugs that took up the vibration'.

Finally set up, the band rehearsed *China Boy* and *Sugar*. Then, Condon recalls, 'Rockwell came out of the control room smiling. Eddie asked, "How were the drums?" Rockwell nodded towards Krupa. "Didn't bother the equipment at all," he said. "I think we've got something." '

The next day, the band cut the two tunes they had rehearsed and a week later were back to record *Nobody's Sweetheart Now* and *Liza*.

Gene and the jazziest jerseys in Chicago in the 1920s.

40

Mezz Mezzrow's recollection of these sessions (obviously a mite hazy since he placed them all on the same day) included the comment that Gene's cymbals were not coming through clearly enough and he had to hold them closer to the microphone with Gene leaning over to strike them when required. Eddie Condon, always the master of the laconic putdown, remembers the second of the two sessions slightly differently but acknowledges that they couldn't have made it without Mezz who helped out when a drum bracket broke away. 'He held Krupa's drum.'

Although Baby Dodds and others had possibly already used well-muffled bass drums on records (sometimes recording engineers insisted the drummer should sit outside the studio door), this use of a full drum kit was certainly a first for OKeh. The drums were so well recorded and played that interested reactions were aroused all across the country. Most importantly for Gene Krupa's burgeoning career was the fact that for many he was the star of the proceedings. As Richard Hadlock comments: 'The records made a favourable impression on Eastern jazzmen, most of whom had not realized how much the Chicagoans had improved. The biggest suprise was Krupa, an unknown, whose well-recorded drum work on these sessions rocked the New York jazz cliques, and ultimately unseated Vic Berton as their chief percussionist.'

Gene returned to dance-band work, playing with one or another of the Benson Orchestras, before a further record date allowed him and the rest of the gang to prove that the first session was no flash-in-the-pan.

In April 1928, calling themselves the Chicago Rhythm Kings, a group of Chicagoans recorded for Brunswick who were using superior equipment to that used by OKeh. On this date Muggsy Spanier replaced McPartland and Mezz was allowed to play tenor in place of Bud Freeman. Red McKenzie sang one song and Eddie Condon another, although as he readily admitted later he shouldn't have perpetrated such an unwise act. Once again, Gene's playing was impressive and proved to anyone who cared to take notice that he was now a major force in jazz drumming.

Many did choose to take note, not least those 'back-East' musicians who had been so impressed with that first record date.

But this was Chicago, and while it might be the place where new and exciting things were happening on the jazz scene, it was not the Big Apple. Reaching the top in any branch of show-business, the movies excepted, meant making it big in New York.

In 1928, during one of its periodic but usually short-lived purges, the Chicago Police Department closed down some of the city's clubs. While this was not enough to cause panic it did help make up the minds of a few who were being tempted to try their luck in New York.

Red McKenzie had already convinced Eddie Condon that they should go. Red's connections, which had allowed him to convince OKeh that they should record the Austin High Gang, were as good back in New York as they were in Chicago. But the real impetus for the others came with a tentative offer of a job. This was from a singer named Bea Palmer who was well-known on the Chicago club circuit and who enjoyed the music played by the crowd that frequented the Three Deuces. Bea landed a job for herself at the Chateau Madrid in New York and persuaded her new boss, Lou Schwartz, that he should hire the Chicagoans. She introduced him to Eddie whose account of the meeting suggests that Schwartz was not as convinced as Bea thought. At another of his clubs Schwartz talked with Bea and Eddie and she asked if he'd heard their records. 'Yes,' Schwartz said, as if admitting that he'd beaten his wife. 'Aren't they wonderful?' she demanded. 'Wonderful,' Schwartz said sadly. However, it was enough for Eddie to head back to Chicago and round up a few of the boys.

Unfortunately, Bea Palmer's marriage, which was a long-running on-off affair, went into one of its off moments. As her husband, Al Siegel, was also her stage partner, this presented a problem. Eddie effected a reconciliation of sorts when both Bea and Al turned up in Chicago. Everything looked set and goodbyes were taken.

Mezz Mezzrow's recollection in his autobiography was that everyone was ashamed to be deserting the real jazz scene of Chicago for the bright lights of show-biz in New York. Mezz reiterates his role in the developement of Gene Krupa's style, and adds similar comments about how he had 'spent a lot of time coaching Joe Sullivan too, giving him little hints I'd picked up from Tony Jackson, Earl Hines and all the other great Negroes who had ever grabbed a handful of keys'.

Despite a session at a night club called the Nest where, according to Mezzrow, the band leader, Doc Poston, sang a preaching blues with lyrics tailored to remonstrate with the gang for leaving poor old Mezz behind, Eddie Condon soon returned to New York. With him went Frank Teschemacher, Joe Sullivan and Gene Krupa and they move into the Cumberland Hotel across the street from the Chateau Madrid. McPartland and Freeman telephoned and were brought up to date. They were touring with the Ben Pollack band and had found themselves playing alongside a new trombone player named Jack Teagarden and wanted him to join the gang. All looked set. Then Bea Palmer came into town, but without Al Siegel. Lou Schwartz didn't want Bea without Al and he certainly didn't want the Chicagoans without Bea.

Eddie and the gang now realized that however much an impression they had made back in Chicago, and even if their records had been well-received by the New York jazzmen, as far as the Big Apple's club scene was concerned, they were also-rans. Eating became a problem but they played in their hotel rooms and word spread. They were hired by a society bandleader to play as the alternate band at a ball for some Newport blue-bloods. It was quite an experience. As Eddie recalls, 'Every name was a foot long; I was surprised that anyone ate with his own hands.' Expected to play waltzes, the band set up and Eddie looked around, 'Krupa was adjusting a tom-tom. The artillery was ready. "Well," I said, "let's give out with some of that old world atmosphere . . . " ' and they launched into *Clarinet Marmalade*.

The society musicians enjoyed this new raw sound. As for the blue-bloods, they were certainly intrigued. 'They couldn't talk,' Eddie remembers, 'because we were playing too loud; between sets we pushed them out of the way to get at the free champagne. "Extraordinary demonstration of the freed libido," I heard one matron mutter. "Lady," I said, "will you hold this glass while I get some caviar?" "Extraordinary creature!" she said, but she took the glass and held it while I got some eggs.'

Another job found the gang accompanying ballroom dancers Barbara Bennett and Charles Sabin at the Palace. The review in *Variety* concluded that the dancers were not very good, while the musicians formed 'the poorest seven-piece orchestra on earth'. Fortunately, the gang's spirits were revived by *Billboard* which found them 'commendable'.

Faced with a hotel bill, they 'owed an interesting sum, ninety-nine dollars', and living on a diet of canned tomatoes for breakfast and the free cherries and olives that came with their drinks, Eddie managed to organize a record date with Tommy Rockwell at OKeh. Condon, Teschemacher, Sullivan and Krupa formed a quartet and they made two sides after which Eddie promptly showed Rockwell the bill. He advanced them $100 (against a session fee of $150) which they gave to the hotel clerk. Holding the one dollar change, Eddie asked what they should spend it on. 'The vote was unanimous—canned tomatoes.'

But if work and food were hard to come by, there was an

abundance of musical sustenance to be had in New York. And for jazzmen, it was to be found uptown in Harlem.

Hot music had been a part of the New York scene for many years. Before World War I two important cabaret stars were Vernon and Irene Castle (he came from Norwich, England) and they employed the musical talents of James Reese Europe, a black musician whose career blossomed during the war when he directed the 369th Infantry Band that took European capitals by storm (and fought well too, the 369th Regiment were known as the Hellfighters). Europe taught the Castles some dance steps which he in turn had learned from W. C. Handy. After some polishing, the Castles introduced the foxtrot to the world's ballrooms. Vernon Castle did not survive the war, dying in an airplane crash in 1917 (he had enlisted in the Royal Flying Corps). James Reese Europe was not much luckier. Although he came back from the war, his career was halted in 1919 when he was murdered by his band's drummer.

Thanks to the Castles, to Jim Europe, and to such popular song writers as Irving Berlin, the musical tastes of many New Yorkers were soon slanted towards black music, albeit usually in much-diluted form.

In the heart of Harlem, however, dilution was not necessary. Seventh Avenue, between 131st and 139th, and Lenox Avenue, between 140th and 145th, were hot-beds of jazz. For the Chicagoans, the realization that their own District was, for all its proliferation of clubs, comparatively small beer was an eye-opener. There were Connie and George Immerman's Connie's Inn, Barron Wilkins's Inn, the Kit Kat and the Oriental Cafe, Ed Smalls had the Paradise (complete with a variable apostrophe), there were the Yeah Man and Herman's Inn, the Nest and the Harlem Uproar House, the Sugar Cane, Pod's and Jerry's and Dickie Wells's club, the 101 Club, Capitol Palace and the Black Cat, the Lenox Club and the Rhythm Club, and, most famous of all, the Cotton Club at the corner of 142nd and Lenox.

The musicians to be heard, either formally playing the clubs or gathering for after-hours jam sessions, included Duke Ellington and most of his sidemen, among them Johnny Hodges, Sonny Greer, Harry Carney, Barney Bigard and Tricky Sam Nanton. There were Tommy Ladnier and Jimmy Harrison and Bobby Stark. New Orleans-born guitar-player Danny Barker recalls in his autobiography an occasion when he visited the Rhythm Club. On this particular day, it was a Monday afternoon: 'Most of the famous leaders, stars and sidemen were there—the big names I'd heard and read about: Benny Carter,

Don Redman, Horace Henderson, Fess Williams, Claude Hopkins, Sonny Greer, John Kirby, Johnny Hodges, Freddie Jenkins, Bobby Stark, Chick Webb, Big Green and Charlie Johnson.'

It was inevitable that the young Chicagoans would wallow in such an excess of musical talent. 'There was a constant search for a new kind of music,' Gene Krupa would recall, 'and it was important to listen to everyone—Fats Waller, Zutty, Tatum, Louis, Willie "The Lion" Smith, Chick Webb—no matter what the instrument or the style. I always felt that going uptown was like taking a lesson.'

Henry 'Red' Allen, in conversation with Whitney Balliett, recalls white musicians who 'came up from downtown to sit in or listen: Jack Teagarden and the Dorseys and Krupa and Red Nichols and Goodman and Bunny Berigan'.

The Harlem theatres were similarly well-stocked with extraordinary talent. The Lafayette, on Seventh Avenue at 132nd Street, was known as 'the cradle of the stars' both for the newcomers who began their careers there and for its endless stream of established highly talented singers, dancers, musicians, comedians and all-round entertainers: Bessie Smith, Mamie Smith, Maxine Sullivan, the Mills Brothers, Ethel Waters, Lil Hardin, Jackie 'Moms' Mabley, Stepin Fetchit, Bill 'Bojangles' Robinson, Leadbelly, Bennie Moten, Duke, Jimmie Lunceford, Fletcher Henderson, Earl Hines, Claude Hopkins. Later, in 1934, the manager of the Lafayette, Frank Schiffman, and his partner, Leo Brecher, moved out and bought the old Hurtig and Seamon's Music Hall on 125th Street. Renamed the Apollo Theatre, this new venue became the topmost rung in black theatreland. To play there was accolade enough; to play there and succeed in winning over the notoriously hard-to-please audience was a seal of approval throughout show business.

Not far beneath the Apollo in status were Loew's Victoria and the Harlem Opera House which were also on 125th. The audiences for the Apollo and its kin were largely, if not exclusively, black. The clubs and cabarets were a different matter. While segregation was not overt, many encouraged white patronage while others, in a kind of retaliation, catered almost entirely for blacks. The attraction of the cabaret was expressed (not too clearly) by Ellin Mackay, the daughter of a wealthy Long Island family, in a letter to the *New Yorker* in 1925. 'We go because we prefer rubbing shoulders in a cabaret to dancing at an exclusive party with all sorts and kinds of people.' Miss Mackay, who later married songwriter Irving Berlin, went on to state that the cabaret was 'a realm of privacy, removed from the institutional demands of [our] social group, community opinion, and family constraints'. Well, whatever Miss Mackay thought she meant by all that, she, like many others of her social group, helped turn Harlem into an in-place for the in-crowd.

The appeal to the white socialites was not jazz. Nor was it always the high standard of other forms of entertainment on offer in Harlem. For many, black entertainers were somehow untouchably exotic. To such people, although they heard jazz and the blues in Harlem, it was more important that they should be seen. Harlem was 'in' and snobs always gather in such places.

The black clubs apart, there was still plenty on offer to New York's nightclubbers. There was Mary Louise 'Texas' Guinan, who greeted patrons of her club with the heartfelt cry of 'Hello, Sucker!' Jimmy Durante's club featured the act of Clayton, Jackson and Durante. A young lady, a descendant of Polish immigrants, hailing from Milwaukee, came to New York via Chicago where she had scandalized night-club audiences with her provocative dancing. Renamed Gilda Gray, and with Sophie Tucker's backing, she danced the shimmy, a torso-shaking dance which originated with black performers, to the delight of the New York set.

But snob appeal was not what kept jazz musicians going uptown. they went because, quite simply, the music there was the best. In between starving quietly in their hotel rooms, Eddie Condon, Gene Krupa and the gang were forever hanging out uptown.

By now Gene had developed from a pleasant-looking, rather skinny youth into a young man with matinee-idol good looks. Early publicity photographs, taken before tousled hair became part of his image, reveal a striking resemblance to the movie actor Tyrone Power. He was still slim, thanks to the cherry and olive diet, but although short in stature, 5' 7" or so, he was broad-shouldered and muscular; his drumming saw to that. Sadly, as his friend Eddie Condon recalled, around this time he was called to Chicago when his mother fell sick but Ann Krupa died while her not-yet-famous son was still on the train.

In March 1929 Eddie had managed to scare up a record date for himself on which he played with Fats Waller. One of the earliest integrated recording sessions, it was also highly successful (even if, as Eddie recounts, the band was assembled an hour-and-a-half before the session was due to start and the tunes 'rehearsed' in the cab as they drove to the studio). On 18 April trumpet player Red Nichols headed a band at a

With such a resemblance to movie star Tyrone Power it was not surprising that Hollywood beckoned—or that several female movie stars began taking an interest of a different kind.

recording session in which he had Benny Goodman and Gene Krupa recording together for the first time. Later that year, on 30 September, another date with Fats was also integrated. This time the band included black New Orleans clarinet player Albert Nicholas, white trombonist Jack Teagarden, and Gene.

One month later, on Tuesday, 29 October 1929, came the stock market crash. For those who had wanted to see, the warning signs of the Great Crash had been there for some time. Falls in prices had been followed by repeated recoveries, which gave an illusion that President Herbert Hoover might be right

Gene Krupa

100% Slingerland EQUIPPED

when he swept the country in the election of 1928 with the prospect of 'four more years of prosperity'. The following years, as America slipped into the Great Depression, had far-reaching effects (even the jazz world would be affected) but it did not hit everyone. Up in Harlem, stocks and shares didn't mean too much. As Jervis Anderson has written, 'There was no distance in American life greater than the few miles from the centre of wealth and possibility downtown to the black district in uptown Manhattan—which people were already calling a ghetto, and where the majority of the residents were poor. So to most Harlemites what the newspapers were calling Black Tuesday looked to be very much a white occasion.' It was a short-sighted view. Later, as the Depression bit, Harlem was affected more than any other district of New York. By 1930 half of Harlem's 200,000 residents, most of them black, were on relief.

Unemployment did not pass unnoticed but, despite its rise, the nation's leading businessmen were not alarmed. In 1930 one of its organizations, the National Economic League, placed unemployment eighteenth on their list of problems facing the nation (way below law and order, Prohibition, international stability and the like). A year later, unemployment had risen to fourth place but was still behind law and order and Prohibition. Of course, the worst was yet to come.

For musicians this was a time for worry. While they were not untouched by the Crash, nor yet by the incipient Depression, it was the usual problem of finding an opening which they faced. True, there was work to be had if they looked for it. Apart from the cabarets and clubs, there were dance halls and theatres. As Samuel Charters and Leonard Kunstadt observe, the white musicians in New York were more haphazard than those in Chicago and were scattered thoughout hotel and pit bands playing for revues and vaudeville. But they would gather in hotel rooms, listen to records and jam. 'They were young, irresponsible, and carefree. They were too wrapped up in their music to care about much of anything else.'

One musician who kept going with a steady stream of the more commercial jobs was Red Nichols, and Gene Krupa worked with him on a number of occasions. One such job found him in the orchestra pit for *Strike Up the Band*, which ran for 125 performances at the Times Square Theatre from January 1930. Alongside him in this band were Benny Goodman and trombonist Glenn Miller. The show's composer was George Gershwin and, despite Gene's inability to read music, he was able to offer constructive suggestions. Fed up with playing a corny four-bar solo on temple-blocks the arranger had written into the score, he suggested to Gershwin that they use the 'freeze beat'. This was a musical device he had seen used to good effect by Duke Ellington at the Cotton Club. The freeze beat is a sudden pause which focuses the audience's attention and which provides a moment of dramatic tension. Although it subsequently became a standard feature of stage musicals, it was then quite new. Gershwin was sufficiently impressed to ask Nichols to include Gene in the band for his next show. As John Hammond has observed, thereafter Gene 'was always George Gershwin's favourite drummer'.

This next show was *Girl Crazy* which opened at the Alvin Theatre in October 1930. In the cast was leading lady Ethel Merman and a young newcomer, Ginger Rogers. Charlie

Teagarden, Jack's trumpet-playing brother, was in this band and so, too, was Miller who obligingly helped Gene overcome his musical illiteracy by cueing him in.

While working on *Girl Crazy* Gene was staying at the Dixie Hotel in Manhattan. The telephone operator at the hotel, charged with the task of giving Gene his morning call, was Ethel Maguire. He liked her voice and one day, when a pretty, brown-eyed, chestnut-haired young woman was pointed out to him as being his regular caller, he asked for a date. It was love at first sight but, despite the comparative regularity of pit work, marriage was not yet on the cards.

Another job, in 1932, was with Russ Columbo for whom Benny Goodman was the contractor. This entailed hiring and rehearsing the band, a task for which the steely young Benny was more than adequately equipped. While on this job Benny and Gene had a minor clash over the small matter of whether Gene should use brushes or sticks on a particular number. Benny won the clash and earned Gene's displeasure. (Columbo, a popular crooner of the day, died in 1934 of wounds received while cleaning a gun.)

There were regular recording dates now, many of them under Nichols's direction. Records by Red Nichols and his Five Pennies (a name which frequently hid almost double that number of musicians) proved very popular and there is no doubt that Gene and Teschemacher and other Chicagoans helped ignite the sometimes slightly ponderous playing of both Nichols and Miff Mole, another of Red's regulars. Gene was also hired for a recording date led by Benny Goodman and set for 27 November 1933. On this date, the small band accompanied a new and very nervous young singer. She sang one song and three weeks later came back to record another with the same group. Neither performance lit any fires but later Billie Holiday transformed not only jazz singing but the whole of American popular song.

By now, Gene's playing style had changed. The slight stodginess of the Baby Dodds style was lightened by snappy rim-shots (most commonly achieved when the drumstick simultaneously strikes the drum head and the metal rim) and by a more flowing rhythm which resulted in part from a shift to 4/4 time. Gene's new mentors were the black drummers he heard in Harlem, among them the flamboyant Big Sid Catlett and Cuba Austin who was with McKinney's Cotton Pickers. His major influence, the last to seriously affect him in his development, could also be heard in Harlem: Chick Webb.

Visually, there was another change which dramatically affected Gene. Formal tuition under drum teacher Stanford

Moeller gave him a new approach which favoured flailing arm movements. The generally accepted role of the drummer as a barely-seen figure at the back of the bandstand was being changed. This new technique, allied to those already strongly developed shoulders, arms and wrists, allowed Gene to create prodigious volume. Most significant for his future fame, it gave him a dramatic, if flashy, visual style. (It was one which he wryly acknowledged on more than one occasion when needing a pseudonym for recording dates: he chose 'Chicago Flash'.)

His development continued when he finally decided to learn to read music. It was a timely decision for just around the corner lay the era of the big bands. Also imminent was the repeal, after thirteen years, of Prohibition, that great American social experiment which had become a thoroughgoing social disaster; and now, no longer possible to ignore, came the full weight of the Depression.

These events, while unrelated, combined to influence the course of popular music in America and as Leroy Ostransky observes 'materially affected the employment of musicians. Big-band jazz, for example, could not have reached its peak during the early 1930s if employers had been required to pay musicians enough to live on. Willing to play for two or three dollars a day, musicians eagerly sought work. When Prohibition ended, the subsequent boom in nightspots offering music provided job opportunities. And the nightclubs and theatres prospered for not all the rich had lost all their money in the stock market crash of 1929.'

Repeal was ratified on 5 December 1933, and for those who could find something to celebrate they could now, at least, do so within the law. For those who stayed home, there was entertainment to be heard over their radios. This was still a massively growing audience. From 12 million families in 1929, the figures zoomed to 28 million by 1939 (around 85% of the population).

Significantly, the nation's musical tastes changed. John Chilton writes: 'It appeared that the majority of ballroom-dancers had tired of the vigour and intensity of jazz and were reflecting what seems to be a twentieth-century trait, favouring sentimental and uncomplicated music during times of stress.' Chilton cites the attendance records at a Harlem ballroom in 1932; the top five bands were white, commercial dance bands. Fortunately, there were still places where jazz was wanted. One, far enough away to be ignored by most but to have an important effect upon the later fame and fortune of Benny Goodman and Gene Krupa, was Europe, and England in particular. Closer

MAL HALLETT AND HIS ORCHESTRA
1933.

to hand was the Savoy Ballroom in Harlem, and that too affected Gene.

Gene had continued to find work. Just as he had in Chicago, where he never let his desire to play jazz overwhelm his need to eat, he took jobs with any commercial outfit that would hire him. The earlier Columbo job had been in New York but he also played with Irving Aaronson in Chicago and Mal Hallett at Atlantic City (Jack Teagarden was in this band), and in view of the regular work he and Ethel decided to marry. They took rooms at the Landseer Apartments, something which came to the attention of Eddie Condon. One night, he and Max Kaminsky were locked out of their hotel room (for the customary non-payment of the bill). Having heard that Gene had opened with Buddy Rogers, Eddie called him. ' "Sorry to bother you, Gene," I said, "but Maxie and I have just been locked out of the Lismore and we wondered . . ." ' Krupa interrupted me.

Mal Hallett towers over his band at Atlantic City's Steel Pier in 1933 where, five years later, Gene would unveil his own band. Left to right: *Skin Young, Joe Carbonero, Frank Ryerson, Mickey McMickle, Jack Jenney (an unsung giant of the trombone), Spud Murphy, Cliff Wetterau, Gene, Pete Johns, Ollie Ahern, Frankie Carle, Vic Mondello, Jimmy Skyles, Toots Mondello, Mal Hallett.*

"Come right down," he said. "I'm sorry I haven't a better place, but this was all we could find. I'll fix the day-bed for you in the living-room and leave the door open." He waited up for us, gave us a drink, and tucked us in.' (In recalling this story, both Condon and Kaminsky state that Gene and Ethel were on their honeymoon but their marriage took place in June and Eddie's version has him and Max freezing in February. Poetic banjo-player's licence, maybe.)

The Buddy Rogers job was heavy-going for Gene. Rogers was an entertainer who had made some movies (and in 1937 would marry Mary Pickford after her divorce from Douglas Fairbanks). Despite hiring a 16-piece band, Rogers insisted on playing a solo on every instrument himself. He was less than pleased when Gene offered to teach him a real drum solo.

But Gene was pupil too, this time informally, to a master technician who was at home in a small group, could play quite extraordinary and spectacular drum solos, and who could supercharge a big band, to say nothing of electrifying the crowds at the Savoy Ballroom. He was Chick Webb.

The Savoy had opened back in 1926 and quickly became known as Harlem's 'shrine of the public dance'. Owned by Moe Gale, a white man, and managed by Charles Buchanan, who was black, the Savoy was a truly marvellous place. The relative decorum of a marble staircase and cut-glass chandeliers was countered by an orange and blue colour scheme. Half the floor was carpeted and scattered with tables, chairs and settees. There was a soda fountain, two bandstands on a revolving stage which allowed the music to be continuous thoughout the long nights, and there was the dance floor itself, 10,000 square feet of polished maple-wood flooring.

The first bands hired for the Savoy were Leon Abbey and the Savoy Bearcats, and Fess Williams and his Royal Flush Orchestra. But from the time he first played there, Chick Webb, a tiny, crippled hunchbacked young man from Baltimore, became King of the Savoy. During the 1930s, as the newer free-wheeling musicians came into New York from Oklahoma City and Kansas City (particularly those who were associated with Count Basie), they devastated the other Big Apple bands but, despite the band 'battles' which were a regular feature at the Savoy, no one ever unseated little Chick. With the infectious and unflagging, swinging beat he generated, and to which the dancers at the Savoy responded excitedly, it was not surprising that the place became known as the Home of Happy Feet. (One decidedly dubious source attributes the origin of this tag to a comment made by movie star Lana Turner.)

Chick Webb, the tiny king of the Savoy.

Gene listened to Chick and learned (and would later engage him in a battle), and quite marked changes took place in his playing style. Before coming to New York he had mixed the fiery Chicagoan approach with the solid New Orleans drum methods; to this he had already added a crisper technique. Now he added another ingredient, a dynamic fluidity which reflected Chick Webb. While he would only rarely reach Chick's heights, the overall standard of his playing rose strikingly. But the kind of job he was forced into taking prevented him from achieving any real recognition, or indeed, as he still wanted to play jazz, any true satisfaction. Fortunately, even if the nation was entering the depths of the Depression, musically speaking Herbert Hoover's prediction was finally coming true and good times really were just around the corner.

CHAPTER 3

SWING IS HERE
FAME AND FORTUNE

'For all that Benny did for music, for jazz, for musicians, and for me, I, for one, doff my cap in a salute of sincere appreciation.'
Gene Krupa

The earlier comment, that the two major factors in the rise of the big-band era were the repeal of Prohibition and the nation's headlong rush into the mass unemployment of the Depression, holds good but there were others. Paradoxically, despite the rise in unemployment, in some quarters there was more money about. In those parts of the nation less severely affected by the Depression there was even money to be spent on entertainment. Some of it went in the direction of one or another of the proliferation of dance halls, at concerts, theatres, the movies, or simply on gramophone records.

Theatregoers, especially in New York, were not merely entertained, they were also educated in political reality. The Group Theatre produced a string of highly successful plays including *Golden Boy* and *Waiting for Lefty* and the Group's nucleus of writers, directors and actors later went on to success in Hollywood: Clifford Odets, John Garfield, Lee Strasberg, Luther Adler, Frances Farmer, Elia Kazan. Not surprisingly, given their radicalism, many also later fell foul of the establishment and were hounded from their jobs. There was also the Federal Theatre where Orson Welles experimented with controversial productions (including, in 1936, an all-black version of *Macbeth*).

Moviegoers laughed at the Marx Brothers and at the slick and sophisticated Thin Man comedies with William Powell and Myrna Loy. Their box-office dimes turned a moppet named Shirley Temple into a millionaire before she was six, and they saw, in 1933, the incomparable debonair skill of Fred Astaire as he and Ginger Rogers went *Flying Down to Rio*. There was serious fare too with the first anti-war film since the ending of World War I, *All Quiet on the Western Front* (1930), and a powerful recreation of the world of the gangster in *The Public Enemy* (1931) and *Scarface* (1932). The coming of talking pictures had not fully uprooted the tradition of live music at the movie theatre. A feature film and a live orchestra on-stage were standard fare, and musicians consequently benefited.

Records sold in ever-increasing numbers and it was no longer necessary to own a record player (although many did) for this was the era of juke boxes which spread across the country until seemingly every bar, wayside tavern and diner had a gleaming glass and chrome musical monster in one corner. The records featured jazz, dance music and popular songs of the day. Some songs reflected the times: *Brother Can You Spare a Dime, Ten Cents a Dance, Gloomy Sunday* (which was imported from Hungary where, it was reputed, several people had committed suicide after hearing it); other songs brightly contrasted the times: *Life Is Just a Bowl of Cherries, Beer Barrel Polka.* For the most part, however, popular composers of the 1930s went about the business of creating a huge catalogue of songs, many of which were masterpieces and have since become 'standards': *Night and Day, Easter Parade, I Got Rhythm* (from the show, *Girl Crazy*, where Gene Krupa had 'educated' George Gershwin on the dramatic possibilities of the freeze beat), *Three Little Words, Anything Goes, Pennies From Heaven, Love Walked In, Stormy Weather* (written for a Cotton Club show), *Cheek to Cheek, Solitude.*

Most people, however, still found their main source of entertainment on the radio which was to many families what television would be a generation later. Although radio was primarily a source of entertainment, its power for political purposes was discovered. President Roosevelt established the 'fireside chat' as a means of drawing closer to the people, and Father Charles E. Coughlin, the Detroit 'radio priest', spoke weekly to more than 20 million listeners with what Cabell Phillips has called 'an appealing blend of radicalism, political extremism, common sense, and often incomprehensible economics'. And, of course, manufacturers and marketing companies discovered the power of radio for advertising. Soon everything from breakfast cereals to hair oil, automobiles to cigarettes, biscuits to beer, was being advertised and the sponsor became a highly significant factor in the development of American popular culture.

Radio also provided musicians with an increasing number

What the well-dressed Man About Drums is wearing this year.

56

of employment opportunities. Ultimately, it gave the rising interest in big bands a final boost which launched the Swing Era, made millionaires out of many—notably Benny Goodman—and brought to national eminence a hundred or so musicians, mostly white. One of them was Gene Krupa.

Benny Goodman had been working more steadily than most, thanks to his technical ability which allowed him to play any kind of music in any kind of band. His ability as an organizer had not gone unnoticed and he was frequently called upon to act as contractor (as with the Russ Columbo band where he had had a minor altercation with Gene Krupa). But he was growing weary of being only the straw boss. In his growing ambitions, Benny was aided and abetted by John Hammond who, in 1931, had unearthed a special interest in Benny in England. Recording sessions had followed, including the Billie Holiday debut and a set with Jack Teagarden as featured singer. Krupa was involved in both sessions although the argument with Benny still rankled. As John Hammond recalls, Gene, usually easy-going, was adamant. 'I'll never work for that son of a bitch again. When he hired me for the Columbo band he would only let me play with brushes.'

In 1934 Benny was persuaded by his brother Harry and pianist-raconteur Oscar Levant to form a band to audition for a new supper club in Manhattan. This was Billy Rose's Music Hall. The band was good and, fortunately, was recorded during its brief existence. Its demise came about when Billy Rose, who was a reformed bootlegger, was eased out by new management. Benny and the band went too. This band (which did not include Gene Krupa although he was on some of Benny's 1934 recording sessions) gave Benny the taste for leading a big band. But where could he get work for one?

For a while it looked as if John Hammond might have the answer when a European tour was mooted for a multi-racial dream band. This was to comprise Red Allen, Doc Cheatham, Bill Coleman on trumpets; J. C. Higginbotham, Jack Teagarden, Will Bradley, trombones; Benny Carter, Edgar Sampson, Chu Berry, and Benny himself on reeds; a rhythm section of Teddy Wilson, Laurence Lucie, Hank Wayland and Gene Krupa; the whole deal rounded off with Bessie Smith. But a dream is what it remained when the British end of the proposed tour hit insurmountable snags.

With Benny about to give up, another audition arose, this time for a new radio show. The National Biscuit Company was planning a three-hour dance-music show to be broadcast on Saturday evenings. The sponsor's plan was to feature three

Before their smashing success the Benny Goodman band plays for the 'Let's Dance' programme in December 1934.

bands; the first slot would go to the sweet style of Murray Kellner; the middle hour to Xaviar Cugat's rumba band; and the show would end with a hot band. It was for this slot that Benny auditioned. At this time the Music Hall band's personnel had undergone some changes but Benny was still unhappy with drummers Sammy Weiss and Stan King. As he later recalled, 'There was only one drummer at that time who would fill the bill, give the rhythm section the lift it needed. That was Gene Krupa.' In stepped John Hammond again. Gene was with Buddy Rogers in Chicago but was still not happy at the prospect of playing under Benny's leadership. Hammond persisted, telling Gene that Bunny Berigan had been hired for the trumpet section and that the band would be playing arrangements by the great black bandleader Fletcher Henderson and, hopefully the clincher, Gene would be featured. As Hammond recalls, 'At that point Gene had to play for the floor show, during which

Buddy Rogers went through his usual act, playing a variety of instruments, each worse than the last. At the next break Gene returned to my table and said, "All right, John, I'll come." '

No one can seriously doubt the importance of Gene Krupa in the success of Benny Goodman's band (even if success did not come at once). He brought with him a committed enthusiasm which few bandleaders got from their sidemen. As Benny would recall many years later, 'The way he fussed and worried over it, you would have thought that it was his band.' Musically, Gene's aggressive Chicagoan-based style pushed Benny along to hot performances of the kind he occasionally made on some Red Nichols records but could all too often subordinate to his technically brilliant, but sometimes clinical, approach to music. Then there was the all-stops-out volume with which Gene played and which jolted the Goodman band along with an urgency none of his successors achieved. Visually, there were all the flashy tricks of Chick Webb and Sid Catlett, magnified a few times (and not always with their impeccable swing), and there was his dominating, grunting, sweating, gum-chewing presence, accentuated by the high arm action taught him by Stanford Moeller. All these facets of Gene's work, his glowing personality (which contrasted strikingly with Benny's sometimes dour appearance), helped boost the Goodman band. Ironically, it was these very same characteristics which would later cause the split between Gene and Benny.

The Nabisco show, entitled 'Lets Dance', ran from 1 December 1934 until 25 May 1935 and the consistent work allowed the band to settle in beautifully. By the time the show closed, Benny and his managers thought he should take the step up to a swish hotel engagement. The chosen venue was the Grill Room at the Roosevelt Hotel in New York; it couldn't have been a worse choice. The patrons had previously been lulled over their dinners by Guy Lombardo and his Royal Canadians whose gentle style, 'the Sweetest Music This Side of Heaven', was as far removed from Benny's band as it was possible to be. On opening night, with the waiters indicating their feelings by walking around with their fingers in their ears, it came as no surprise, if a major disappointment, when the band was promptly given two weeks' notice to quit.

The band made several excellent recordings, many of which used Fletcher Henderson's superb arrangements. A national tour was set up but before they left Benny and Gene made some records with pianist Teddy Wilson. Benny had met Teddy at a party at the home of singer Mildred Bailey. They had played together, accompanied by Mildred's cousin, Carl Bellinger, and struck up an immediate musical rapport. The record sessions duplicated this, with Gene replacing young Carl on drums. The Benny Goodman Trio was thus born and their first sides quickly proved to be enormously popular with the record-buying public. But the fact that Teddy was black meant that, for a while, recording studios were the only place they played together.

The band left on its tour and played a succession of dance dates in places like Pittsburgh, Columbus, Lakeside, Toledo and Milwaukee, each one seemingly worse than the last. Sometimes, the public didn't want to know; other times, it was the promoter. At Elitch's Gardens in Denver, in the Rocky Mountains, customers asked for their money back while the owner objected to the fact that the tunes lasted too long. At three dances for a dime, he wanted a faster turnover. Benny argued, as only Benny could, but backed down on his manager's advice and played two-minute waltzes from borrowed charts. By the time they reached California, Benny was ready to quit. He doubtless concurred with Wingy Manone's remark, 'Man, good jazz just can't make it over them tall Rockies.' But Gene was one of those who urged Benny on, pointing out that he had left a steady, better-paid job for the chance to play jazz.

An engagement at Sweet's Ballroom in Oakland was nowhere nearly as bad as their earlier experiences. Here, the people were standing in line before the dance was due to start. What none of the band had allowed for, in arriving at their estimates as to how the tour would fare, was the time-zoning of the United States and the effect this had upon the audience for their NBC 'Let's Dance' broadcasts. As Benny later explained, 'The show had been broadcast from 11.00pm to 2.00am, New York time. That meant it reached the West Coast between 8.00 and 11.00pm or at the best possible time in which to develop an audience. So, when we got to the Coast, they were ready for us.' Additionally, and helping prime Californian teenagers, a Los Angeles deejay, Al Jarvis, had been playing their records on his show.

The band arrived in LA for a one-month engagement at the Palomar Ballroom. Knowing that the management had tried to cancel them after hearing about the difficulties in Denver, the band was understandably nervous. They cautiously played all their sweeter tunes. The audience looked a bit askance and applauded politely. Then Benny, thinking that this might be the end of the road, called for Henderson's arrangement of *King Porter Stomp* which featured a red-hot Bunny Berigan solo. This was what the fans had come to hear and the roof came off.

The month-long gig was extended before the band was allowed to begin its return swing across the country to New York. If the outward leg had been a depressing catalogue of failure, their return was a triumphant procession. Not that too much word went ahead. At each new venue the band had to prove itself but, brimming with confidence, they did so with considerable flair. Most successful of all was their stopover at the Congress Hotel in Chicago. Recently reopened after a food-poisoning scare during the World's Fair, the hotel wanted exposure. It certainly got it. For almost six months, the Benny Goodman band attracted rave notices and was heard by millions on live radio broadcasts. For at least two members of the band, Benny Goodman himself and Gene Krupa, both now twenty-five years old, to make it so big in their home town was sweet indeed.

Relaxing during the Benny Goodman band's sensational engagement at the Palomar in Los Angeles in 1935. Left to right: Bill De Pew, Jess Stacy, Harry Goodman, while Gene studies his fan mail.

A foretaste of the coming integration in Benny's organization came when Fletcher Henderson's band arrived in town to play at the Grand Terrace. The Chicago Rhythm Club, one of whose moving spirits was Helen Oakley (later to marry British jazz writer and critic Stanley Dance), suggested some kind of cooperative venture. Benny and Gene went along to the Grand Terrace and played a few numbers with the Henderson band.

As Benny recalled, 'This was probably the first time that white and coloured musicians had played together for a paying audience in America.'

Back in New York, the band was on the brink of even greater successes, although no one had yet fully realized just how much their music had taken hold of the younger generation.

The hard slog of the past year took its toll and Gene was briefly hospitalized. In January 1937 he replied to a letter written to him by a British fan, Wellington B. Holliday,

Gene prepares to cool off during the 1935 trip to sunny California. Harry Goodman appears to be taking bets on his survival.

confirming that he was now back with the band and fully recovered. It was just as well, for the breakthrough in LA and in Chicago was about to be repeated in New York.

Booked into the Hotel Pennsylvania, the band was also to double at the Paramount Theatre in Times Square as the live music half of the customary movie plus live music show. At 6am on 3 March 1937 there were already 1,000 fans waiting in line; by 7.30 police were needed, and when the doors were opened (at 8am) 3,634 paying customers flooded in, leaving almost the same number disappointed outside. Inside, when the movie eventually began (it was *Maid of Salem* with Claudette Colbert) no one took much notice. When the band appeared there was uproar. 'That reception,' said Benny, 'topped anything we had known up to that time, and because it was spontaneous and genuine, we got a tremendous kick out of it.'

Despite realization of their new popularity, it was some time before it fully sank in. For the first time, jazz musicians were

63

revered as if they were movie stars or sports personalities. High on the list of favourites was Gene Krupa. Indeed, in individual terms he was much more popular than was Benny Goodman. There is no mystery to this. For those fans who had only records or radio broadcasts to go on, he could be heard playing with all stops out on all but the softest of ballads. For those who also saw him live at dance dates, he provided an astonishing spectacle.

From this point onwards, like it or not (and there were many dissenters), the drummer was no longer an anonymous figure hidden behind a mountain of equipment at the back of the band. After Krupa, the drummer was as well-known and as dominant as a front-line man, a major soloist, and often the most popular with the crowds (who were not, by and large, discerning jazz fans). Interestingly enough, the popularity of drummers on the fringes of the jazz world was not entirely unknown. Back in

Just one of many venues where the Benny Goodman band met with acclaim in 1936. This one is the Stanley Theatre in Pittsburgh, Pennsylvania.

65

1915 Earl B. Fuller, drummer with the Banjo Wallace Orchestra, had attracted considerable attention, if mainly for his $1,000-worth of equipment which, the press hastened to tell its readers, occupied 64 square feet of floor space. Earlier still, around 1908, during the Broadway run of *Miss Innocence* starring the popular Anna Held, the pit-band drummer was required to give a roll on the drums as the curtain went up. One night the curtain stuck, and with commendable presence of mind he went into a long solo while the stagehands struggled. He received such an ovation that, from then on, he was required to play a long solo every night.

The earlier jazz drummers, such as those from whom Gene Krupa had drawn his first inspiration, were capable of skilled and rhythmic solos (as both Baby Dodds and Zutty Singleton have demonstrated in live performance and on record), but considered their role to be primarily, sometimes exclusively, that of providing a rhythmic base for the other musicians. Later giants, many of them contemporaries of Krupa's, like Dave Tough, Chick Webb, Big Sid Catlett, and Jo Jones, extended

Gene with two of Benny's trumpet stars: Harry James and Ziggy Elman.

Two of the Famous Four: Lionel and Benny.

the drummer's role to provide the major element of swing in the rhythm section and to listen to, cushion, and lift the soloist. In some near-telepathic cases, especially Catlett and Jones, the drummer would anticipate where the soloist was going next and be ready to propel him forward. Krupa was only rarely on a par with such musicians, and even at his best he never came close to Jo Jones. But Gene and the host of imitators who were soon to be seen in many of the white bands of the Swing Era did bring dash and spectacle, adding visual excitement to the musical thrills. Unfortunately, in some cases, spectacle was all there was. Sadly, there were times when this was true in Gene's case and gave rise to the sometimes widespread assumption that this was always so. However, as Charles Wilford observes in Stanley Dance's *Jazz Era: the 'Forties,* 'In spite of appearances his drum solos were logical and rather economically constructed, always remaining pieces of jazz for one instrumentalist, instead of degenerating into mere technical displays.'

On 4 May 1937 the Benny Goodman band clashed with Chick Webb's outfit at New York's Savoy Ballroom. Later, Gene conceded that the tiny Chick had won the battle but from the sweat-stained jacket it must have been some scrap.

As previously suggested, of the superior black drummers, the one Krupa most closely resembled and upon whom he openly remodelled his style, was Chick Webb. On one night, 4 May 1937, the Goodman band ventured into the Savoy Ballroom where little Chick held sway for one of the periodic band battles the patrons there loved so much. As Gene later recalled with typical generosity, 'That man was dynamic; he could reach the most amazing heights. When he really let go you had a feeling that the entire atmosphere in the place was being charged. When he felt like it, he could cut down any of us.' And Chick did cut down Gene. But most of Gene's fans were white kids from middle-class homes and they didn't frequent the Savoy. In their world, Gene was the tops. A fact which was becoming increasingly and irritatingly apparent to Benny Goodman.

Benny was frequently a martinet and every musician who

ever played with him has a story about his apparent lack of emotion or fellow-feeling. Yet, for all his personal flaws, Benny possessed real courage which manifested itself with his hiring of Teddy Wilson in 1936. Those records of the Benny Goodman Trio had proved so popular that after some persuasion from Helen Oakley and the ubiquitous John Hammond, Benny took Teddy on as a regular member of the entourage. Once Teddy was hired, Benny stuck it out through the first awkward months. The integration of a black musician into an otherwise white group was eased by Teddy playing only with the Trio and not with the full band. Later, when Benny, Teddy and Gene jammed with Lionel Hampton at a Los Angeles club, a similar arrangement took place. First, Lionel made some records, then he joined the organization, but only as a member of the Benny Goodman Quartet.

Gene with critic, jazz-writer, pianist and composer Leonard Feather in the mid-1930s.

Given the racial tensions which existed in America in the 1930s, the step taken by Benny and a few others during this period (Artie Shaw hired Billie Holiday; Lena Horne worked with Charlie Barnet; June Richmond with Jimmy Dorsey) must be seen as one of considerable courage and determination. It also set markers for Gene Krupa who would later make his own statement on the subject.

The Benny Goodman band's popularity reached its peak during 1937 and when impresario Sol Hurok suggested a concert at Carnegie Hall Benny allowed himself to be persuaded. (The fact that at regular intervals in his career Benny was 'persuaded' to do things suggests a weak-willed man. In fact, he was so positive and hard-headed that it is more accurate to suggest that when he wanted to do certain things he occasionally needed the comfort of the conviction of others.)

Although it was widely held to be the first jazz concert at Carnegie Hall (which was America's most prestigious classical

music venue), there had been previous performances there of popular and jazz-fringe music. Nevertheless, this was the first occasion when an uncompromisingly jazz-oriented programme was presented. A date was set, 16 January 1938, and tickets were swiftly sold out. (The Hollywood version of this event, in the 1955 movie *The Benny Goodman Story*, ludicrously had the hall packed with the highbrow set. It was, of course, the band's fans who bought tickets.) After a slightly shaky start, the band came together after an explosive burst from Krupa's drums which raised the first roar of approval of the evening. By the end, after sparkling (if sometimes nervously too fast) performances by the Trio and the Quartet (and a jam session which featured several leading black musicians culled from the bands of Count Basie and Duke Ellington), the fans were ecstatic. When Gene pounded his tom-toms to signal the band's regular closing number, *Sing, Sing, Sing,* they went wild.

Hooray for Hollywood! Gene was with Benny's band in the 1937 movie Hollywood Hotel *along with singers Frances Langford and Dick Powell.*

It didn't much matter if, musically speaking, the show was stolen during this tune by the band's pianist, Jess Stacy, who performed a piano solo of startling originality and grace in the midst of the thundering drums and screaming brass. The lasting image of the occasion, both visual and aural, was of Gene Krupa, jaw chomping as he perspired his way through long, explosive drum passages. As Stacy observed to Whitney Balliett, 'Gene was our salesman, our showman, and he worked hard. You could wring water right out of his sleeves when he finished a set.' Not surprisingly, for the fans Gene had done it again. Unfortunately, for Benny the limit had been reached.

Never one to willingly share the spotlight, Benny found Gene's popularity rankled. But there was much more to it than simple jealousy. Benny's musicianship was always a critical factor in his approach to his work. He was clearly conscious of how the qualities of the Fletcher Henderson arrangements they played were sometimes lost under his band's steamrolling approach. Other arrangers aimed more towards what the Goodman band really sounded like with Krupa on drums; Henderson's earlier arrangements had been written for his own band (and the difference between how the two bands sound on the same arrangement is striking) and even those specially written for Goodman require a looser style.

Benny later remarked that he always had problems with drummers, although his hiring of Big Sid Catlett in 1941 suggests that his troubles were often self-induced. Despite his extraordinary swinging musicianship, nowhere in jazz was there a greater gallery-pleaser than Big Sid. Not surprisingly, Catlett soon moved on. In 1959, Benny hired Dorothy Dodgion who one night received overwhelming applause. 'When I came off,' she recalled for Sally Placksin, 'Benny's manager says to me, "Bye." I got my notice the next day. As Gene Krupa once told me, "Just remember, baby, he's fired the best." '

After Carnegie Hall, Benny began to pull back on Gene's excesses. He wouldn't let him solo as often as he had, and when he did bow to the fans' wishes he adopted an attitude of studied boredom. Rumours of a split spread. For a while they were quelled and even those closest to the source thought all would be well. As George T. Simon, one of the leading writers on the big band scene of the day, wryly observes, even he got it all wrong. ' "Chances are you'll be hearing all sorts of rumours that Gene is planning to leave Benny tomorrow or the day after," I wrote in the March 1938 *Metronome*. "The chances are even greater that these rumours won't be true and that Gene will continue to chew gum in the back of Benny's stand for a while to come," I added reassuringly. A sad seer I proved to be: the day after the issue hit the stands, Gene Krupa left Benny Goodman after a blowup at the Earle Theatre in Philadelphia.'

They soon repaired their friendship. As Benny stated in his

The Benny Goodman Quartet: Lionel, Teddy, Benny and Gene.

*One of the all-time
great jam sessions.
Randall's Island, New
York, in May 1938
where thousands of
fans were entertained
by dozens of bands in
an open air jazz
festival. Here Gene
lays down the beat for
trombonists Bruce
Squires and Dalton
Rizzotto and
trumpeter Dave
Schultze while Eddie
Condon clutches his
throat in anticipation
of opening time.*

autobiography, 'For just about the three most important years of my life Gene plugged along with me, taking the breaks as they came, working as hard as any man could.'

But, if their friendship survived, musically they were now on different tracks and apart from guest appearances on each other's radio shows they would not meet as regular co-performers for a quarter-century.

Clearly, neither man was unprepared for the split. Within days Dave Tough was in Benny's band (and making it sound lighter and more swinging even if the fans demanded that he play his solos like Gene). Unfortunately, Dave's drinking had become a problem and he didn't last long with Benny's demands for propriety and reliability. After Dave, and such short-lived occupants of the drum-chair as Sid Catlett, the only drummers to bring an effective presence to the Goodman band and survive Benny's basilisk eye were Nick Fatool and Roy Burnes.

For his part, Gene had already commissioned arrangers to prepare charts for a band of his own and was scouting musicians. A few weeks after he had quit Benny's band he was ready to unveil his own.

In those few weeks before the first public appearance of the new Gene Krupa band in Atlantic City on Saturday, 16 April 1938, a considerable amount of feverish activity took place. Gene's lawyer-manager, Jerry Gluskin, took care of the organizational details, musicians were hired, arrangements made and copied, uniforms provided, music stands made, bookings arranged, and he coped with all the countless odds and ends which Krupa the sideman had taken for granted. As Gluskin commented, 'The formation of a band is more than a musical problem. It's a financial problem. It's an organizational problem.' And like all such problems, there were times when it all seemed too much trouble, especially when the fans, too, seemed to take it for granted.

When a band eventually makes its appearance on-stage, everything appears so polished and well-organized that the fans may be forgiven for overlooking the long hours of blood, sweat and tears that have gone before. As Gluskin remembered, 'Like almost every bandleader before him, Gene was ready to throw up the sponge a hundred times. On the train down to Atlantic City, he reached the zero hour. He was certain that the band would be a "bust"—and had to be prevented from turning back to New York.'

Gene need not have worried. Even if, musically, the band had a long way to go, the fans had no doubt that their hero had made the right move. George T. Simon's rave review in *Metronome* carried a headline that told all: 'Krupa's Band Kills

Cats At Atlantic City Opening—Felines Howl, Then Purr. As Gene's New Gang Blasts Forth At Initial Siege.'

But, for all the enthusiasm of the fans (some 4,000 of them crowded into the Marine Ballroom at Atlantic City's Steel Pier on that April evening), the band did have some musical problems. The brass and rhythm sections were in pretty good shape but the reeds were weak and, greatest problem of all, there were too few good jazz soloists in the ranks. Tenor saxophonist Vido Musso, poached from Benny's band, was an exception but most of the others were sectionmen at heart and failed to provide the inspired spark that was needed to lift the band above the average. Most at fault, however, was Gene himself. Most of the band's new arrangements featured his drumming and, while the fans loved it, any chance for the band to improve was halted. With hindsight it was possible for Gene to acknowledge this fact. This qualification apart, the arrangements were otherwise very good. In the first few years he used charts by such experts as Jimmy Mundy, Chappie Willet, Elton Hill, Adrian de Haas, Buster Smith, Dave Schultze and George Sivaro (who played trumpet and alto saxophone respectively in the band), Benny Carter and Fletcher Henderson himself. Yet despite the quality of the arrangements, the band lacked a distinctive sound and, when not featuring Gene, could be easily mistaken for an average local outfit on a good night.

Personnel changes gradually improved the band. Sam Donahue's arrival greatly improved the saxophone section even if it meant the loss of Vido, and Corky Cornelius proved an asset to the trumpets as did Shorty Sherock. Other improvements to the initially weak reeds came with Sam Musiker and Clint Neagley.

The standard practice of having a pretty girl singer with every big band of the Swing Era often led to leaders hiring second-rate canaries who chirped away less than adequately at intervals throughout the dance dates. For his pre-opening record dates, Gene borrowed Helen Ward from Benny Goodman. (The harsh words spoken at their bust-up were forgotten and when both bands happened to be in Philadelphia in May, the two leaders took the opportunity to make their reconciliation public—and found time to play a game of baseball.) For his first singer, Gene hired Jerry Kruger whose Billie Holiday-inspired style did not sit too well with the fans. He replaced her with Irene Daye who was a little better than average and featured on one of the band's earliest hit records, *Drummin' Man* and the later success, *Drum Boogie*.

At the Atlantic City opening, a young male singer had joined the band in the hope of being hired on a permanent basis. Within a couple of months Gene did hire him. Leo Watson was black, and decidedly different from the usual run of singers, male or female. Putting it mildly, the fans were sometimes puzzled by his rare brand of scat singing. This was in the days before scat became an accepted part of popular singing style. Today there are Ella, and Sarah, and Mel Torme, and countless others. Then there was Leo Watson. If hiring Leo was unusual because he was black, musically speaking it was positively adventurous.

Gradually, Gene saw the error of too many drum solos. As

Gene prepares to give the downbeat to his trumpet section. Left to right: *Shorty Sherock, Torger Halten, Corky Cornelius and Rudy Novak.*

one ballroom manager pointed out, 'Gene, you're a good kid, a nice boy, and a hard worker, but even the *Super Chief* stops once in a while.' The sheer physical effort was draining him. Louis Zito, Gene's road manager for many years, has spoken of this to Rudi Blesh and others. 'No one goes near Gene for at least half-an-hour after a stage show. He's completely exhausted and soaked to the skin.' Despite a hearty appetite, Gene never put on weight, losing three pounds a day due to his performances.

On the road, the band met with mostly praise and approval from the fans. They played the Glen Island Casino, New York's Roseland and if they laid an egg in Cleveland, then so, too, did several other big bands of the day.

Life on the road was tough. The Hollywood cliche of happy musicians playing merrily as their bus cruises along open roads contrasts sharply with the reality of overcrowded coaches, punctures and mechanical breakdowns, snowstorms and floods,

detours, overnight hops of 300 miles and more, ragged nerves
from too little sleep, inadequate food at all the wrong times,
too many cigarettes, too much booze. Gene recalls, 'That life
was so full of greasy spoons and bad food. You yearned for a
night off, and when you got it you'd get so drunk you wouldn't
know what was going on anyway. I used to look at the lighted
windows of the houses and yearn for the same kind of life.'

In an attempt to put down roots, Gene and Ethel bought a
plot of land in Yonkers, New York and built a house there. Ethel
sometimes travelled with Gene, as she had when he was with
Benny, and, as George Simon reported in *Metronome*, she had
been the most excited person at the Atlantic City opening and
'just kept on smiling and beaming all night long'. But there
were strains on the marriage, some caused by the long stretches
on the road, some by the temptations that lay along the way
which were not always resisted.

Gene's favourite open-air relaxation was always baseball although here he looks as if he's on the losing team. That may be Ray Biondi hiding beneath the cap.

Undoubtedly, Gene's band was hugely successful. His name
was enough to guarantee full houses wherever he appeared.
In *Metronome's* poll the band was listed while he topped the
drummer's list, beating his old Chicagoan friend Dave Tough
and white New Orleanian Ray Bauduc who was then with Bob
Crosby's band. He wrote a regular column, 'Drummer's Dope',
for the same magazine; and an instruction book, the *Gene Krupa
Drum Method*, was published, as was a note-for-note
transcription of his work on *Sing, Sing, Sing*.

Conga-drumming up the beat at the 1939 New York World Fair.

He also contributed an article for *Rhythm* magazine in May 1939, in which, before going into detailed recommendations for up and coming drummers, he advised on the need for balance in drumming. 'Without balance, you cannot hope to get rhythm, or that solidity of tempo which is so vitally necessary to the modern-day swing orchestra . . . ' Developing this thought, he continues, 'If your right hand has more power than your left hand, you are going to have a jerky beat. This will show itself either by a racing, or a dragging, tempo which no amount of hard work on the part of the musician can correct.'

Hard work was a constant factor in keeping himself and the band in the public eye. Gene's popularity made an invitation to Hollywood a safe bet. During the Swing Era, many of the most famous bands of the day were hired for fleeting appearances in feature films. Gene had already appeared in movies with Benny's band and now it was his turn. In his case, however, the moviemakers decided to entrust him with rather more than a brief bandstand sequence. In 1938 he worked with Bob Hope and Shirley Ross on *Some Like It Hot*, taking third billing and turning in a commendable acting performance. Musically, he contributed to the film's title song (with Frank Loesser and Remo Biondi, the guitar-player in the band), and also with performances on-screen of several of the band's best-known tunes including *Wire Brush Stomp* and *Blue Rhythm Fantasy*.

To be actually appearing in the movies seemed to Gene and

BOB HOPE · SHIRLEY ROSS · GENE KRUPA AND HIS ORCHESTRA

SOME LIKE IT HOT

with UNA MERKEL · RUFE DAVIS

Screen Play by Lewis R. Foster and Wilkie C. Mahoney · Based on a Play by Ben Hecht and Gene Fowler
Directed by George Archainbaud · · · A Paramount Picture

SWING (continued) Page 60

HERE ARE 30 GOOD HOT RECORDS

LIFE has compiled, from considered opinions of experts, a list of good swing records. Printed below, they form the nucleus of a good collection for those who would like to know more about hot music. The list does not include hard-to-get collectors' items. All these disks can be bought at stores which keep a fairly complete hot stock. Included are some items of special interest like the Beiderbecke piano solo (Bix was almost as good on the piano as on the horn) and the freak swing success, *Flat Foot Floogie*.

ALBERT AMMONS, PIANO: "BOOGIE WOOGIE STOMP"; DECCA 749

LOUIS ARMSTRONG, TRUMPET: "WEST END BLUES"; OKEH 41078

MILDRED BAILEY, VOCALIST: "'LONG ABOUT MIDNIGHT"; VOCALION 3378

BIX BEIDERBECKE, CORNET: "RIVERBOAT SHUFFLE"; COMMODORE 29-30

BIX BEIDERBECKE, PIANO: "IN A MIST"; OKEH 40916

BUNNY BERRIGAN, CORNET: "I CAN'T GET STARTED"; BRUNSWICK 7945

CONNIE BOSWELL, VOCAL: "BOB WHITE"; DECCA 1483

EDDY CONDON'S WINDY CITY SEVEN: "CARNEGIE DRAG"; COMMODORE MUSIC SHOP 1500

BOB CROSBY'S BAND: "SOUTH RAMPART STREET PARADE"; DECCA 15038

TOMMY DORSEY, TROMBONE: "STARDUST"; VICTOR 25320

DUKE ELLINGTON'S BAND: "CLARINET LAMENT"; BRUNSWICK 7650

ELLA FITZGERALD, VOCAL (CHICK WEBB'S BAND): "A-TISKET A-TASKET"; DECCA 1840

BENNY GOODMAN, CLARINET: "DON'T BE THAT WAY"; VICTOR 25792

BENNY GOODMAN QUARTET: "MOONGLOW"; VICTOR 25398

FLETCHER HENDERSON, BAND: "MONEY BLUES"; COLUMBIA 383 D

GENE KRUPA, DRUMS: "BLUES OF ISRAEL"; PARLOPHONE R 2224

MEADE LUX LEWIS, PIANO: "YANCY SPECIAL"; DECCA 819

JOE MARSALA, CLARINET: "HOT STRING BEANS"; VOC. 4168

RED NORVO, XYLOPHONE: "BLUES IN E FLAT"; COL. 3079

KING OLIVER, TRUMPET: "DIPPER MOUTH BLUES"; OKEH 4918

ARTIE SHAW, CLARINET: "NIGHTMARE"; BRUNSWICK 7965

BESSIE SMITH, VOCAL: "YOUNG WOMAN'S BLUES"; COMMODORE MUSIC SHOP 5-6

STUFF SMITH, VIOLIN: "YOU'SE A VIPER"; VOCALION 3201

JOE SULLIVAN, PIANO: "HONEYSUCKLE ROSE"; COMMODORE MUSIC SHOP 31-32

JACK TEAGARDEN, TROMBONE: "DIANE"; COMMODORE 505

FATS WALLER, PIANO: "DINAH"; VICTOR 25471

TEDDY WILSON, PIANO: "BODY AND SOUL"; VICTOR 25115

MARY LOU WILLIAMS, PIANO: "OVERHAND"; DECCA 781

MAXINE SULLIVAN, VOCAL: "LOCH LOMOND"; VOC. 3654

SLIM AND SLAM, VOCAL AND DOUBLE BASS: "FLAT FOOT FLOOGIE"; VOCALION 4021

B. BERRIGAN

E. FITZGERALD

F. HENDERSON

T. WILSON

J. MARSALA

M. BAILEY

S. SMITH

C. BOSWELL

F. WALLER

G. KRUPA

M. SULLIVAN

SLIM & SLAM

others like him nothing more than a natural progression from their present status. The movie-star treatment the major stars of the Swing Era received had given many musicians a strange sense of their own importance. The adulation of fans, access to politicians and movie stars, the sudden leap in income for the bandleaders and all the temptations of wine and women that came with it, proved too much for some. Even if Gene had such unremarkable hobbies as those claimed by the fan magazines (collecting cigarette lighters and playing with his Scottish terrier), he soon learned how to spend money a shade more spectacularly. His wardrobe expanded theatrically, and he would tour with three trunks filled with custom-made clothes. If the sweat and strain of his performances justified a regular turnover in shirts and suits, the fifteen camel hair topcoats were something else. However, he never lost sight of the fact that his success was due to his fans' acclaim and always remained highly approachable.

But, domestically, matters were not good and by 1941 the Krupas' marriage was foundering and Gene and Ethel parted. At bottom, the problem lay in the fact that Ethel was very much the girl-next-door and despite her obvious love for Gene was never at ease in the environment in which they now moved. When the divorce eventually came it was as amicable as such things can be, and Gene settled $100,000 dollars on Ethel, a substantial sum in those days. Perhaps if they had been able to have children matters might have been different, but Gene could not. As he would later reveal to Bobby Scott, this was not merely an emotional matter but one which concerned him deeply as a Catholic.

There was romance on the road, however, and it had its effect upon the Krupa band's personnel. Corky Cornelius and Sam Donahue were both interested in Irene Daye and when Corky quit the band to join the Casa Loma Orchestra, Irene made her choice. She went with Corky, they were married and had a child (Corky died in 1943 when only 29).

Losing a good trumpet player and a good singer at the same time could have been a damaging blow. In fact, it turned out to be the best thing that could have happened for in replacing Corky and Irene, Gene acquired two people who transformed his band and made it, for the first time, an organization worthy of the name he alone had hitherto enjoyed.

Some time before Irene quit, Gene had heard a young singer who had greatly impressed him. The young woman had utterly failed to impress Benny Goodman, who dismissed her from an audition for failing to stick to the written melody. But Gene

Hamp the Champ

heard in Anita O'Day's strongly jazz-oriented approach to singing something that he wanted. He promised Anita that if he ever had a vacancy, she could fill it. Anita took him at his word and hung on to one dead-end singing job after another waiting for the moment.

Anita very quickly became a superb asset and anything but the pretty canary hopping out to warble a swift song before being swept off-stage again. For a start, Anita chose not to look like all the other girl singers. A strikingly attractive woman, she was soon dressing in a tailored uniform just like the boys in the band (a decision which led to unwarranted rumours about her sexual proclivities). But it was in her singing style that she was most different. Of all the white singers in jazz, Anita is the one whose sound comes closest to the best black singers. Even if some critics were slow to spot her ability (Barry Ulanov suggested in *Metronome* that she 'should clear her throat'), the more perceptive soon realized that hers was a major talent.

Gene and an almost obscured Charlie Christian help drive the 1940 Metronome All Stars from a distance. Included in the band are bass-player Bob Haggart and three reeds: Eddie Miller, Benny Goodman and Benny Carter.

Joining Krupa at this moment in her life was a major decision for Anita and one which entailed considerable fortitude. Her frequently harrowing account of her life in her autobiography conveys in explicit detail what she went through in order to take the job with Gene. Her book also vividly conveys her impressions of Gene when she went along to the Chicago Theatre in Chicago a few days before she was due to join the band. 'Gene was as magnetic as a movie star, filled with wild exuberance as his raven-coloured hair, flashing brown eyes and black suit contrasted with the snow-white marine pearl drums that surrounded him. His gum-chewing, facial gymnastics, tossing of broken sticks to the audience and general flamboyance visually complemented the Krupa sound . . . I'll never forget the sight and sound of him as sweat popped from his forehead, ran down his face, dripped off the tip of his nose, moistened his flying hair and came through his shirt as his arms flailed in twenty directions to produce different musical sounds.'

Anita's first gig with Gene's band was at the University of Michigan on 14 February 1941. Unfortunately, no one had taken the trouble to discuss music with Anita and had assumed that she would simply take over the songs that Irene had been singing. Of the existing arrangements, the only one within Anita's compass was *Georgia On My Mind* and she was so successful that first night she had to sing it three times.

Very quickly, Anita developed a full library of songs with special arrangements for her unusual talents. 'She could sound like a jazz horn,' said Gene. She also developed a reputation as a lady with a wicked line in wisecracks. Since she was the only woman in the crew still more rumours flew, these directly contradicting those about her sexual preferences. But she was not prepared to hop casually into bed. As she remembers, Gene sat next to her on the bus one night. 'He began to move in and very casually asked: "How would you like to have breakfast with me?" "Sorry," I told him. "I never mix business with

Gene and his band backing the unlikeliest singer of them all: Barbara Stanwyck, star of the 1941 movie Ball Of Fire. *Roy Eldridge is second trumpet from left.*

pleasure." "Good girl." A few minutes later, he said he guessed he'd try to get some sleep. I never had any more propositions—if it was one—from Gene. I was glad. I liked Ethel.'

A couple of months after Anita joined the band, Gene hired a new trumpet player. He had known and admired Roy Eldridge for some time. Roy—for many the link between Louis Armstrong and Dizzy Gillespie—was, and remains, a powerful and dynamic performer. If he is occasionally flashy, he is always capable of playing with dramatic intensity. 'I dug this guy,' Gene has commented, 'dug his playing so much.' Gene and Roy had met during the days when Gene was scuffling in New York and Roy was playing uptown in Harlem.

Gene caught up with Roy one night and talked casually for a while. Gene was unwilling to come straight out with an offer because at this time Roy was leading his own small band and he didn't want to offend him by offering a job. But Roy made it clear that his feelings on the matter were reciprocal.

Well, blow, blow, Roy, blow! Anita O'Day urges Roy Eldridge along in the best band Gene ever led.

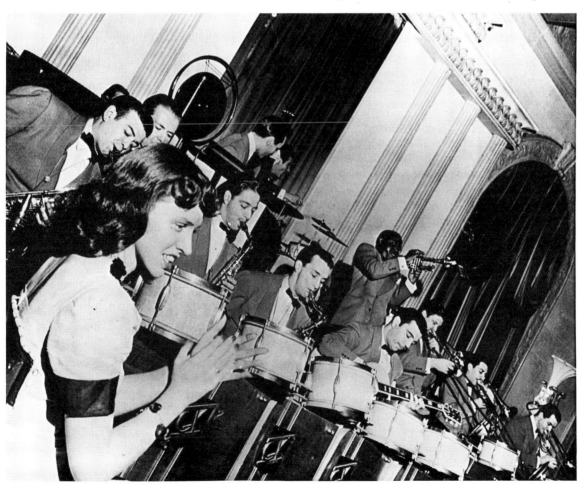

Financially, it made sense, too, for Roy would get more playing with Gene than leading his own band in clubland. Of course, both men knew that there were potential problems. Despite Benny Goodman's hiring of Teddy Wilson and Lionel Hampton, the sight of black musicians with white bands was still a rarity. They decided to ease Roy in the way Benny had done with Teddy and Lionel, by featuring him as a special soloist. Very soon, however, all pretence was dropped and Roy took his place in the trumpet section. He was also featured on some numbers with Anita. Her cry of, 'Blow, Roy, blow,' was taken up by the fans and, aided by new arrangements and a new spirit among all the musicians, they helped build Gene's band into one of the best of its time and certainly the best band he ever led.

For Roy Eldridge, being with the band caused mixed emotions. At first, he recalls, 'It killed me to be accepted as a regular member of the band. But I knew I'd have to be awful cool; I knew all eyes were on me to see if I'd make time or do anything wrong.' Certainly, being the only black man in the band gave him some difficult moments. As he later recalled to Leonard Feather and others, there were those days when the band would arrive at a hotel after long hours on the road. The hotel clerk, discovering that the Mr Eldridge on the band's list

Gene celebrates his 33rd birthday at New York's Roseland Ballroom with left to right: Phil Napoleon, Jimmy and Tommy Dorsey, Frankie Carle, Sam Lanin, Jan Garber and Roseland manager Joe Belford. The lady with the big knife is Gene's friend Carol Bruce.

was black, would suddenly find that the hotel was all booked up. Restaurants wouldn't serve him, in some places he couldn't use the washroom. 'By the time that kind of thing has happened night after night, it begins to wear on my mind; I can't think right, I can't play right.' On the ferryboat at Norfolk, Virginia, he and some of the band were on the top deck and were told, ' "We don't allow niggers up here." When a complaint about this remark was made to the captain, he commented: "Well, if you can stand him, it's all right with me." Just as if I had leprosy.'

In time the tensions such treatment generated affected Roy and he became edgy. He and Anita sparred where they had once harmonized. Soon their quarrels began to affect the rest of the band and when Anita decided to quit it came as no real surprise even if it was a huge disappointment.

Before that day came, however, the band went from success to success. Constantly on tour, days and nights ran into one another. Along the way things happened that were good and bad, lasting and transient. There were affairs with the girls met on the road, but they were not all those nameless yesteryear groupies who dog the accounts of many touring musicians. As Anita O'Day remembers, while Gene's fame and fortune were substantial, in the circles in which he now moved many others had as much if not more. His good looks and relaxed charm caught the eyes of attractive ladies who were similarly well-known and wealthy. 'In addition . . . he had a little fling with Dinah Shore and then moved into the big leagues with Lana Turner.' After reputedly being discovered sipping soda at Schwab's Drugstore on Hollywood Boulevard (however improbable, this is a considerably more believable part of her publicity material than that which claimed it was she who named the Savoy Ballroom 'The Home of Happy Feet'), Lana had entered the movies, playing various small roles in which her chief asset, a well-filled sweater, had been shown to good advantage. Nicknamed 'The Sweater Girl', Lana proved very popular with servicemen, who chose her as their favourite pin-up girl. She was equally popular with men closer to home. In 1940, then twenty, she married her first husband, swing bandleader Artie Shaw, and was divorced from him by the time she met Gene. Later, after her very hot affair with Gene had cooled, she demonstrated that, brief as her marriage to Artie was, she had picked up one trait from him. Altogether, at last count, she married seven men (eight marriages), thus closely matching Artie's eight trips to the altar.

After the affair with Lana, Anita reports that Gene's

drinking habits got a little out of hand. He would also make occasional but far from excessive use of marijuana which, Anita remarks, '... made him a lot easier to work for.'

The war had its effect on the band. After Pearl Harbor, the draft was whisking men out of band uniforms and into the khaki variety so fast that as Gene once remarked to Rudi Blesh, 'I only met some of those guys as they came out with a suitcase and said, "Goodbye, boss." '

Among Gene's off-stage duties around this time was one which set a new drum star on the road to fame. In February 1942 Gene, along with George T. Simon, H. H. Slingerland (whose company had provided Gene with his drums in return for the best advertising any musical instrument company could ever hope to have), and Frank Verniere were the judges at an amateur drum contest. The winner was Louis Bellson, then aged eighteen.

Despite the loss of Anita, and his split with Ethel, the future looked pretty good for Gene. But lurking around the corner was a complex affair which would damage him personally, destroy his band, put him in jail, and tag him forever as a drug addict.

Gene can hardly believe his eyes at the unlikely teaming of the two violinists: the incomparable jazz stylist Eddie South and Latin American expert Xavier Cugat. Teddy Wilson is the pianist, John Kirby on bass while Red Norvo sits this one out.

CHAPTER 4

COPPIN' A PLEA
THE DRUGS BUST, A NEW BAND AND THE END OF AN ERA

'The first thing that marijuana does is distort time and time is the essence to a drummer.'

Gene Krupa

The history of jazz is littered with stories of musicians who took to drink or drugs. Their reasons are manifold. Some took that road in the mistaken belief that their performance would improve; others out of boredom or defence against the unusual pressures of their lifestyle. And there were those who simply imitated the actions of their peers and idols.

Inevitably, drinking became a significant feature of the jazz life. The association between jazz and establishments where liquor is sold has been a part of the scene since the beginning. In an atmosphere where social drinking was the norm, musicians would have been less than human had not the majority joined in. Just as social drinking can lead people in all walks of life into a drink problem, so it was with some musicians. A few of those who did become addicted to alcohol happened to be leading figures in the jazz world and consequently attracted the attention of the press to an extent disproportionate to their true significance.

The interest shown by newspapers in those who took drugs was similarly out of proportion, although possibly more understandable in the years before drug addiction became a widespread social problem. Despite a few well-publicized exceptions, hard drug users have not been a major factor in jazz. Many of those who did have a problem later overcame it, with markedly less fanfare: Anita O'Day, Miles Davis, Art Pepper. Some, like Charlie Parker, did not survive the abuse. By far the most common narcotic, especially in the 1930s, was the soft option of marijuana.

Simple reference to song titles which use one or another of this particular drug's many euphemisms confirms its popularity among musicians: *Texas Tea Party, Muggles, Reefer Man.*

In the 1920s and 1930s use of marijuana was not illegal in all parts of the United States. This led to confusion when users toured the country. As is now known, from the late 1920s onwards Louis Armstrong used marijuana almost every day of his life, and possibly knew of its properties even earlier. In November 1930, while working at Frank Sebastian's Cotton Club in Culver City, Los Angeles, Louis was arrested and charged with using the narcotic. Quite clearly, Californian law on the matter cannot have been unknown to musicians. In any event, narcotics usage became subject to Federal law in 1937, six years before Gene Krupa's brush with the authorities.

The precise sequence of events leading to Gene's arrest, trial and imprisonment on narcotics and related charges is difficult to determine with any assurance of accuracy. Stories changed (not least that of a major witness for the prosecution) and Gene's own recollections varied over the years. This may have been simple memory lapse or an adjustment to accommodate changes in public perception of narcotic users.

His own statements leave no doubt that he was a marijuana user at one time. In 1969 he lectured to members of the Deputy Educators Against Narcotics in Mineola, Long Island. Part of his talk, reported by Roy R. Silver for *The New York Times*, confirms his use: 'I suppose like every other kid I thought it would better my playing but that was an hallucination. The first thing marijuana does is distort time and time is the essence to a drummer.' Commenting on hearing recordings of his work while under the drug's influence, he 'found it was pretty bad . . . you think you're beating up a storm, but you're not'.

In 1943, however, even if he was using marijuana, it took second place to alcohol. Few people use narcotics and alcohol simultaneously and, as Anita O'Day confirms, the stress brought about through his marital problems was marked by an increase in his liquor intake.

The draft was not only taking musicians from the ranks of Gene's band. Also drafted was the band-boy who, in one version of the account, bought some high-grade grass for his boss as a farewell gift. The band-boy appears to have been proud enough of his action to reveal the purpose of his purchase. Narcotics investigators heard about it and descended upon Gene's dressing room at the San Francisco theatre where the band was playing. They found nothing because the offending substance was in a coat pocket at Gene's hotel. After the agents had left,

Gene Krupa
Ace drummer Man
& his Ensemble
100% Slingerland
Radio King
Drums and
Tom Toms

and guessing that they would head for the hotel, Gene called the young man who was helping cover the regular band-boy's imminent departure. He told him to flush the marijuana away but, instead, the youth decided to remove the cigarettes from the hotel. He was arrested, the drug found and immediately thereafter Gene, too, was arrested and eventually faced two related charges. One, possession, was classed only as a misdemeanour; the other, contributing to the delinquency of a minor by inducing him to transport an illegal substance, was much more serious.

Apart from the immediate and near-hysterical press response which inevitably coloured the public's view of the case, Gene also had the misfortune to fall foul of a crusading DA. Worse still, he hired lawyer Jake Ehrlich for his defence, unaware that Ehrlich and the DA hated one another and both welcomed the opportunity of a headline grabbing contest. It was Gene's misfortune to become a legal football between these two men.

The case was heard before Judge Thomas A. Foley and part of Gene's testimony, that an envelope containing marijuana was thrust into his hand 'by a stranger at a stage door', helped confuse matters. In the event, on 18 May he was found guilty on the misdemeanour charge and sentenced to 90 days' imprisonment and fined $500. At his 30 June trial on the other charge, a predominantly male jury took little over two hours to find him guilty. At the beginning of July, given the indeterminate sentence of 1-6 years, he was sent to San Quentin, this term to run concurrently with the sentence already imposed and partially served.

In later years, talking with Bobby Scott, Gene recalled his prison term with evident displeasure. One of the guards, determined that Gene's fame would not attract favours, threatened fellow prisoners with serious punishment if they befriended him. Not surprisingly, the result of this threat was that other inmates promptly set about helping him any way they could.

It would be surprising if prison failed to change Gene Krupa. Partly, this was as a result of the enforced regimen, the time to do nothing but think, but there was also his awareness of what was happening outside.

Although the band kept going for a short while under Roy Eldridge's leadership, it soon folded. All the hard work of the past five years, to say nothing of the reputation-building three years with Benny Goodman, had been dissipated and, as far as Gene could see, his career was over. On the credit side, he was assured by many friends, Benny among them, that they were still rooting for him. Indeed, Benny visited him in prison (one of the few musicians to do so, although the fact that he was incarcerated in northern California made him inaccessible to many). Most significant of all, Ethel came to visit. She told him that the $100,000 he had settled on her was untouched and she offered it back to him. As Anita O'Day observes, 'I think that was when Gene grew up emotionally.'

On 9 August, Gene was released on $5,000 bail pending an appeal. When the appeal was eventually heard, the decision on the graver of the charges against him was reversed. Serious doubt was also aired at the strength of the lesser of the charges but by then he had served his time for that offence.

Freed from prison, he had to make some difficult decisions. Convinced that his reputation had suffered so much that he

Gene needed more relief than this when he ran foul of California's narcotics detectives.

Gene with his new boss Tommy Dorsey in 1944

would never again be able to play in public, he returned to his home in New York and, apparently, retirement.

For a short while he studied harmony and arranging but was uneasily restless. Benny Goodman had declared in a *Metronome* interview that, 'Anytime, anyplace, anywhere he wants his old job back, it's his.' Words are one thing, actions often are something else but Benny was serious. First, he called Gene and invited him over to his home to talk and play and then he offered him work.

Benny had temporarily disbanded but was preparing to take a band on the road for a tour of army camps for the USO. Gene went along, and received a tumultuous reception. His response was to play better than ever before. (Recordings made of this band show Gene as close as he ever came to the standards set by his idol, Chick Webb.) This was in September 1943 and in October Benny took the band into the Hotel New Yorker to accompany an ice show, Gene was, however still very cautious of public opinion. Playing for servicemen on camps or in the relatively anonymous setting of an ice-show accompaniment was one thing, the main spotlight was another matter entirely. Some clue of likely response was offered when he played with a band for a War Bond rally in Times Square at the beginning of September. As a headline in *The New York Times* put it,

94

KRUPA DRUMS BOOM $56,000 BOND SALES. He also autographed drumsticks to be sold along with the bonds.

Nevertheless, when Benny announced that the band was set to tour, Gene decided not to take the chance of attracting attention to himself. Instead, he opted to stay in New York and take up an offer to join Tommy Dorsey.

Dorsey's band was playing an engagement at the Paramount Theatre (where Benny's band had confirmed their success back in 1937) and Gene's arrival came at such short notice that he wasn't billed. As the stage rose with the band already playing the opening number some of the audience spotted Gene. Delighted and amazed whispers spread around the theatre and soon everyone was standing, applauding and cheering. Tommy gave Gene a nod and he stood, bowing, still playing but soon crying like a child. Few musicians in the jazz world can have enjoyed such a demonstration of public affection.

When the band began a tour, Gene was happy to go with them, assured now that he had no problems with public response. He stayed with Tommy through to the summer of 1944 but was starting to think of forming a new band. In San Antonio, Texas, word came that his appeal had been successful. With the fillip this gave to his morale, he decided to hand in his notice and go back into the bandleading business.

The big band scene was changing in 1944. Very quickly the changes would become major, and catastrophic to many. Of considerable effect had been the musicians' strike which, for several months from 1 August 1942 kept the bands out of the recording studios. The American Federation of Musicians had for some time been unhappy with the fact that sidemen in bands were receiving only scale payments for recording sessions, some of the results of which were selling millions of copies and making some record companies and bandleaders rich. Additionally, more and more radio stations were dropping live music in favour of playing records and musicians were, thus, facing rising unemployment. The union's boss, James C. Petrillo, wanted the recording companies to set up a fund for musicians and, eventually, when they declined, he called a strike.

In the run up to this withdrawal of labour, recording sessions were hurried through to allow the companies to stockpile. Once the strike was in force and the stockpile diminished as the months dragged by, the record companies devised ways and means of keeping their customers happy. One such method was to record the singers whose popularity was already growing with the fans. Among the band singers who had come up through

VIA ARMY B-17s HOLLYWOOD — GRAND ISLAND NEB. DEC.23RD 1944

the ranks of the big bands were such future luminaries of the popular music scene as Ella Fitzgerald, Peggy Lee, Perry Como, Dick Haymes and Frank Sinatra. Recording with choral accompaniment, they filled the gap and in the process helped change the already shifting taste of the general public. Bands were still recorded for the armed services but the resulting V-Discs were (supposedly) unavailable to the civilian population. (After the war, the masters of these recordings were supposed to be destroyed but, fortunately, this did not always happen.)

Cracks in the record companies' walls appeared after about a year and some of the smaller companies signed appropriate agreements with the AF of M but it was November 1944 before everyone had fallen in line. By then, the ever-fickle public taste had changed and people were no longer as eager to buy big band records.

As Albert McCarthy and other observers have pointed out, the enhancement of the careers of singers was coupled with a

The Band That Swings With Strings all togged up for a visit to a USAF base in Nebraska, Christmas 1944. Among the personnel are Buddy Stewart (lying down), Teddy Napoleon (kneeling), singer Ginnie Powell (to Gene's left), Charlie Ventura, Joe Dale and Ray Biondi (3rd and 2nd from right respectively).

96

rising interest in other musical forms being offered. Among these were 'hillbilly' records, a forerunner of the country and western boom. There was also a revival of the earlier 'race' recordings which now brought to public attention some of the black singers and vocal groups then singing in relative obscurity in clubs. Many such singers laid the groundwork for the acceptance of 'rhythm and blues' (which would, in its turn and suitably 'whitened', make way for rock and roll).

When the new Gene Krupa band could make records, in November 1944, the wider public discovered what those fans who had heard the band in person had already learned to their dismay. From his stint with Tommy Dorsey, Gene had inherited a liking for strings. Billed somewhat optimistically as 'The Band That Swings With Strings' the new aggregation thundered away while frantically sawing violins held things back, or on ballads reduced proceedings to an uninviting blandness. Although Gene enjoyed the experience of this band, which allowed him to play music which vaguely resembled that which he enjoyed hearing in his leisure moments (Ravel, Milhaud, Debussy and the like), it was an expensive indulgence. A big band was hard enough to keep afloat without the expense of an extra ten musicians, especially when they were not contributing anything the public wanted.

The band received some adequate notices, among them *Billboard* which acknowledged that much of the band's live performance was 'strictly for show' and that the 'kids in the audience eat it up as do adults, for it's first class showmanship'. But for all such comments, and a high placing in the 1944 *down beat* poll, the concept of Gene Krupa with strings was not quite right.

Despite its shortcomings, the band made some good records including *Leave Us Leap* which became one of Gene's most popular recordings (and which features a fine example of a 'freeze beat'). The band also made a successful record, *What's This?*, which offered hints of some of the musical changes taking place. This features one of the earliest examples of vocalese, an extension of scat singing in which the singer uses his or her voice (in this case the singers were Dave Lambert and Buddy Stewart) as if it were a horn. Such departures showed that, despite his admitted Kostelanetz complex, Gene was prepared to give other musical forms a chance. During this period Gene's public rehabilitation was enhanced by another movie appearance, this time in *George White's Scandals* (1945), which was made while the band was playing an engagement at the Hollywood Palladium.

Another event in the winter of 1944-45 was an appearance in Los Angeles with Norman Granz's Jazz at the Philharmonic. Granz had worked in the film industry and was behind the making of *Jammin' the Blues* (1944), for many the best jazz film ever. Eager to promote live jazz, Granz was determined to do several things, all of them ambitious. He wanted to transfer the adversarial concept of the after-hours cutting session to the public stage; he planned to use the best musicians available regardless of cost; and he intended to brook no interference from segregationalists. His concerts were to be integrated on and off-stage; his musicians would travel first class and be accommodated only in first-class hotels. Such treatment was rare for whites, it was virtually unheard of for blacks. It is a measure of his determination and commitment that Norman Granz succeeded.

One of the first Jazz at the Philharmonic concerts (the name comes from a failed attempt to get the entire wording of a 'Jazz Concert at the Los Angeles Philharmonic Auditorium' into the available space) had Gene in the rhythm section of an all-star band. He was also a member of a trio accompanying Billie Holiday. Granz's intention to hire the best available talent was clearly in full force from the outset as the rest of a mouth-watering bill included Anita O'Day, Coleman Hawkins, and Kid Ory's band. This one-off appearance for Granz would not be followed up by Gene for a few years.

A decision made in mid-1945, to invite Anita O'Day to rejoin the band, was an excellent idea. At first Anita was not convinced it was the right thing for her to do but on learning from Gene's manager, John Gluskin, that the strings were being dropped and that such formidable talents as Dodo Marmarosa, piano, and clarinetist Buddy De Franco had been hired, she signed up. Recently released from a stint with the Stan Kenton orchestra, Anita enjoyed the change. 'Stanley was a gentleman,' she remarks in her autobiography, 'but working with him was like wearing a tight girdle. Working with Gene made you feel relaxed as if you were lounging around in an old kimono.' Anita remained with Gene until early in 1946 but then was forced to quit by one of the crises with which her career was marked. This was a major emotional breakdown which followed upon the pressures of touring and too readily accessible alcholic and marijuana stimulus. By the time Anita was restored to health, Gene had been forced to replace her with Carolyn Grey.

Around this time Gene hired two musicians who were to have a significant effect upon the band he was leading. One was trumpet player Red Rodney, who was already a devotee of the work of Charlie Parker. (In 1949 Red worked with Parker and had the peculiar distinction of having to 'pass' for black in some Southern towns. This feat was accomplished by Parker billing his as 'Albino Red'.) The other young man Gene hired was nineteen-year-old Gerry Mulligan who played baritone saxophone and, most importantly, brought to the band his exceptional arranging talents. With a few more personnel changes (among them the arrival of Don Fagerquist, trumpet, and Buddy Wise, tenor saxophone, whom Gene poached from Mal Hallett's band) adding to such existing modern thinking

Busby Berkeley did it better. Gene is flanked by Joan Davis and Jack Haley in the 1945 movie George White's Scandals.

musicians as alto saxophonist Charlie Kennedy, the stage was set for Gene's bebop band.

The major shift in musical taste within jazz in the early 1940s was, of course, the coming of bop. Largely developed by the younger generation of black musicians, gathering and playing together in after-hours joints along New York's 52nd Street, bop had several in-built exclusion clauses. Bop frequently excluded the older generation of musicians although people like Benny Goodman would sometimes go along and sit in apparently unaware that the boppers were accommodating them by adjusting their performance to suit. To some extent the public was excluded because much of what the boppers were playing was technically far advanced beyond the relatively simple playing of the swing era bands. There was also some exclusion of whites, although perhaps less than later accounts of this period of jazz might allow.

This was a time when black-white relations underwent one

of their periodic downturns. A riot in Harlem at the beginning of August 1943 was gamely downplayed by the authorities, yet New York's mayor, Fiorello La Guardia, who asserted to the press that this was not a race riot, was obliged to sent 5,000 troops and police into West Harlem and impose a curfew. Ironically, reports in the newspapers appeared alongside advertisements for a new revue at the Hurricane on Broadway at 49th Street. This was *Rockin' in Rhythm* which featured Duke Ellington and his Orchestra. If the real Harlem was an exploding powder keg, the music and stars it had helped generate were still the stuff which audiences wanted to see and hear.

For the moment, then, audiences were not taking kindly to bop. Gene's view of it was more open-minded. Of Dizzy Gillespie and Charlie Parker, he observed that '. . . they sounded pretty nice . . .' He was happy to hire the younger generation of white musicians who were filled with the ideas of bop, remarking that he 'liked keeping up with these young sons of guns'. In more general terms, he was aware that factionalism in jazz was bad for everyone. 'I like bop and I like dixie . . . But let's discourage bad musicianship, and I mean by that mickey-mouse bands. By merely fighting among ourselves, we've given those no-goods just that much more of a chance to get ahead of us.'

Yet for all his willingness to listen to and, as he would soon prove, adapt his band to the new music he was not prepared, or perhaps conceded that he was unable, to absorb the marked changes which bop demanded of the jazz drummer.

Led by Kenny Clarke, and with such notable acolytes as Max Roach and Art Blakey, the drummer's role was altered in all principal respects. Clarke began using off-beat accents on the bass drum, explosions of sound which to the untrained or unadaptable ear sounded irrelevant. In addition to this broken rhythm technique ('dropping bombs') as a means of imparting impulse to a soloist was the shift to cymbals and snare drum of the main rhythmic support for the band.

Such techniques had been pioneered by Jo Jones but this cannot obscure the fact that men like Roach, Clarke and Blakey were making major advances in style. After them, the straightforward swingers could not help but sound archaic and frequently unsubtle. In time, the old methods would enjoy a deserved rejuvenation but in the early 1940s the technique of drummers like Gene Krupa became suddenly old hat.

Gene disliked using cymbals and his drumming behind ensemble passages and soloists alike had continuity and its own integral form. After all the years spent developing his highly personal approach it is not surprising that he failed to adapt to a style which many regarded then as uncoordinated with the rest of the musicians in a band. Yet, for all his unwillingness (or even inability) to play in the new mode, Gene certainly encouraged his young musicans to play as they pleased, albeit within the confines of the arrangements made for the big band. These arrangements, especially those by Gerry Mulligan, were fine pieces of work and resulted in some good (and popular) recordings, among them *How High the Moon* and *Disc Jockey Jump*. Gerry's outspokenness caused some friction when he unhesitatingly bawled out the band, and the boss, over what he thought to be sloppy performances. When he did this in public, he had to go, however reluctant Gene might have been. 'I had to admire that guy, you get too much obsequiousness in this business.' This was 1947, the year that Red Rodney also moved on.

The same year brought about completion of the reconciliation between Gene and Ethel which had begun when she visited him in prison. Bobby Scott has suggested that on Gene's part there may well have been his undoubted awareness that in the eyes of his church he was still married to Ethel and their divorce had placed him outside the fold. In the event, Gene and Ethel remarried and settled into a comparatively stable domestic routine.

In February 1947 Gene engaged classical composer-conductor Leonard Bernstein in a debate in the pages of *Esquire* magazine. The piece was headed 'Jazz Forum: Has Jazz Influenced the Symphony?' and Gene took the negative view while Bernstein argued in the proposition's favour. Opposing prevailing opinion, that composers like Gershwin and Stravinsky and others had taken conscious suggestions from the jazz world, Gene makes a stout argument for his point of view. He doesn't really succeed, partly because he calls in to his support evidence of those composers who have been influenced but have failed in the attempt. He rightly suggests that many of those composers who did make musical acknowledgement of jazz did so without real awareness of the form. 'Many,' he wrote, 'approach the native American idiom, the jazz idiom, with intolerance, even with condescension. They stoop, but not to conquer. And so, they almost invariably make an unholy mess of their attempts.'

Leonard Bernstein's view was similarly equivocal, indeed he begins with the statement: 'There is nothing more provocative and challenging than participating in a debate when one is convinced that both sides are wrong.' With part of his argument proposing that many American (and European) composers have inevitably been influenced by various musical forms, several of which have in their turn been influenced by jazz, Bernstein appears to win the debate. Before that, however, both he and Gene have delivered several hundred words, the profundity of which must have come as something of a shock to those of the magazine's readers who associated the drummer with the seamier side of the jazz life.

On a much lighter side, 1947 saw Gene Krupa as the victim of one of Alan Abel's earliest hoaxes. Long before he became American's leading exponent of the craft, Abel was a student at Ohio State University. Having founded a weekly jazz concert, he occasionally managed to persuade touring musicians to play there. After a mix-up with Gene's manager, which resulted in Abel advertising that Gene would play at the university before a formal deal was worked out, the manager announced that there would be no concert appearance. Abel decided to disagree by the simple, if dubious, expedient of kidnapping Gene. Aided and abetted by a horde of fellow students, among whom were half-a-dozen of the prettiest girls he could find, Abel set out for Gene's hotel.

While the male students set up noisy diversions, the girls managed to persuade Gene into a car which roared off in the direction of the university's auditorium which was already filled to capacity.

Understandably irritated by all this, Gene declared that he wouldn't play or even go out on to the stage to speak to the audience. Abel explained his side of the mix-up with the manager, and then told him how important an opportunity this was to let Gene create a good impression in the public mind which would go a long way to killing off forever the clinging vestiges of the drugs-bust publicity. After listening to Abel, Gene thought for a moment, then declared, 'Right now I'm thinking of summoning my lawyer to start legal action against you . . . and the college. Not to mention a federal charge of kidnapping. While I'm figuring out what to do, why don't you go out there on stage and give me an introduction?'

The occasion ended happily, with Gene participating in a jam session and even the manager arriving, all smiles and good nature.

The late 1940s were proving to be decidedly uncertain times for the big bands which were folding on all sides. Gene hung on, however, and continued playing live dance dates and concerts and recording, although now with a shift backwards from the bop-oriented band. Once more, some of the performances were bland although occasional sessions with some fellow Chicagoans were lively and entertaining.

Gene maintained an optimistic view in an interview with *down beat* in August 1950. 'In certain parts of the country, things are mighty rough, but the overall picture is a vast improvement over the same scene of a year ago. Business has been great . . .' After discussing the new band's book, he added, 'I think that within a year we'll find a demand for bands built along the lines of the old Benny Goodman, Tommy and Jimmy Dorsey, Barnet, Lunceford, Chick Webb, Ellington, and other outfits of that era of the 1930s.' His optimism was ill-judged and later that same year he called it a day and disbanded. A short-lived medium-sized band (a 12-piece group) kept his musical life ticking over until the autumn of 1951, but the days of a permanent Gene Krupa band had gone forever.

CHAPTER 5

SLOW DOWN
THE FINAL YEARS

'. . . I felt too lousy to play. And I was sure I sounded lousy. So I decided to go home.'
Gene Krupa

The big bands never really died, but for a while, especially in the late 1940s and early 1950s, it must have looked that way. With disturbing frequency, trade papers reported one after another leader was disbanding. Harsh economic factors prevailed, making the cost of keeping sixteen or so men on the road an impossible burden. And the audience for the new jazz, bebop, shunned as 'old-fashioned' the musical style that had been the breath of life to the previous generation. Dance halls, once the staple venue for the touring bands, found attendances dropping alarmingly and they, too, folded. In this economically vital area, the bebop bands did not provide a substitute for the big bands. It was not impossible to dance to bop, but it was damned hard.

As for the stars of the Swing Era: Benny and Gene and Harry James, even Duke and Count Basie, and scores of others, they found that, as in all areas of show business, the public is remarkably fickle. They wanted new heroes and for the most part they found them outside jazz. Some jazzmen did gain hero status, but it was in an 'underground' manner as the Beat Generation came along and gave the palm to the Hipsters, the West Coast Cool School and the powerful (and ultimately most lasting) hard bop musicians. The new heroes were Charlie Parker, Dizzy Gillespie, Miles Davis, Thelonious Monk, Bud Powell, Art Pepper, Chet Baker, and countless others. The fact that most had paid their dues in the big bands was beside the point. Before achieving their new status they had left that particular scene far behind.

In time, of course, the durable Ellington and Basie, Woody

Herman and Lionel Hampton and a few others surfaced to reveal to a startled public that the big bands had been there all along. When that happened, it was too late for a resurgence on a similar level to what had gone before and it was, in any case, too late for Gene Krupa to take advantage.

The end of his band was a long way from being the end of Gene Krupa as a performer. In the future, however, apart from occasional special formations, he would work with a Trio and, later, a Quartet. For some dates the small group was the main attraction, for others it was part of Norman Granz's Jazz at the Philharmonic package.

Yet throughout the rest of the decade and all through the 1960s, there was a certain predictability both in performance and in Gene's lifestyle. A glance at a page in his engagement book during this period could have been readily confused with any other.

During the early 1950s, in addition to extensive national

tours, Gene also visited Japan and Scandinavia. The Trio included a piano player (perhaps Teddy Napoleon or Hank Jones) and a saxophonist. Usually this was a tenor (Charlie Ventura, Flip Phillips) but occasionally he worked with an alto (Willie Smith, Benny Carter). Eddie Shu, a multi-instrumentalist was the reed player for quite a while, as was Eddie Wasserman. From 1954 onwards the Trio was uprated to a Quartet with the addition of a bass player (British-born John Drew, Whitey Mitchell).

In March 1953 he came to England with a JATP package and played the Gaumont State at Kilburn, London.

The JATP concerts featured Gene in noisy and somewhat pointless drum battles, initially with the late Buddy Rich. These confrontations gave the fans of the two drummers an opportunity to compare and contrast style and technique but did little to advance the cause of jazz. Later, Buddy would observe that he and Gene never 'thought of each other as being competition . . .' he played the way he played it and I played the way I play it and we tried to do the best thing we could for the art of jazz and the art of drumming'. Nevertheless, Buddy blasted away during these sets and clearly 'won' them. Gene was sanguine about it all. As he remarked to Bobby Scott, 'Anyone playing with Bud is going to get blown away . . .'

In 1953 Benny Goodman approached John Hammond with the proposal that he should manage a tour by a reconstituted Benny Goodman Orchestra. In 1950 Benny had found some long forgotten recordings made on a single overhead microphone of the famous 1938 Carnegie Hall concert. The recordings had been remastered and issued on long-playing records and the evening that had lived in glowing memory was discovered to be just as good as people remembered. The success of the records convinced Benny that there was enough public interest for a tour. Gene and Teddy Wilson were signed up and as many of the originals as possible. Where this was not possible suitable alternatives were found. Cautious about carrying the full burden, Benny made a deal with Louis Armstrong who would join the tour with his All Stars.

As John Hammond recalls in his autobiography, what seemed a marvellous idea on paper, failed to work out in practice. Benny, ever the strict disciplinarian, and Louis, happily extrovert, tangled within minutes of their first meeting at a rehearsal. Although the tour, which had begun with Benny and the band alone, started out well, matters degenerated as soon as Louis arrived. The first joint concert was a disaster with Louis playing for twice as long as he should and Benny losing

Gene and Roy Eldridge dining out in Texas in 1949. Among the onlookers are several noted jazzmen of the previous two decades in the Southwest. At left is Lee Hilliard, saxophonist with the Alphonso Trent band; behind Roy is New Orleans-born trumpeter Don Albert who led a band in Texas; at right is drummer Boots Douglas who led the San Antonio-based Boots and His Buddies. The lady is Della St John and the others include Bubber Bright and Clifford Scott.

his temper. At the finale, Benny was made to look foolish when he anounced Louis who failed to come on-stage. Attempts to placate a now irate Benny barely succeeded as neither he nor Louis seemed able to communicate.

Eventually Benny decided that he really didn't need Louis. The tour would be a success with the Goodman band alone. Then Benny was taken ill. Apparently felled by a heart attack, he was placed under strict medical care, while Hammond and others desperately tried to salvage the tour. With Gene Krupa directing the band, and Louis taking over Benny's chores as emcee the tour continued. When Benny announced his return (he had not had a heart attack, and may not have been sick at all) matters had deteriorated with Louis's manager threatening legal action. The tour fizzled out and a splendid opportunity to re-live the past was lost.

Gene beats it out during the jam session sequence of The Glenn Miller Story.

A night-club gig for the Gene Krupa Quartet around 1954. Eddie Shu plays tenor, John Drew is on bass and the pianist is Bobby Scott who became one of Gene's closest confidantes.

In 1954 Gene added Australia to his touring schedule ('. . . the most enthusiastic audience I've played for.') and also made an appearance in a Hollywood bio-pic about Glenn Miller. In a short night-club sequence he and a handful of others joined Louis Armstrong's All Stars for a jam session in the course of which he and Louis's drummer, Cozy Cole, played a duet. Gene and Cozy also formed an off-screen partnership when they opened a drum school in New York. The school's laudable intention was 'to turn out more musicianly drummers'.

The following year, pianist Bobby Scott, then a teenager, joined Gene's Quartet for an extended engagement at The Last Frontier in Las Vegas. Scott became very attached to Gene and their conversations, which ranged over religion and classical music, formed the basis of Scott's heartfelt tribute to Gene in the January 1984 issue of *Jazzletter*. Additionally, Scott remarked on Gene's solitariness. Even an overt approach from an attractive woman was politely ignored. When Scott wondered aloud at this, to him, strange rejection, Gene replied, 'It'd be wrong, don'cha see, Chappie.'

In part, Gene's attitude stemmed from his increasingly close ties with the church and, more specifically, from the knowledge that Ethel, whom Scott remembers as a strong-minded woman who kept a strict eye on Gene's habits, was gravely ill. She died in 1956.

Scott's comments on Gene's solitary behaviour are endorsed by Dave Frishberg (who played piano in the Quartet in the early 1960s). 'Although,' as Dave recalls, 'I never had much of a personal relationship with Gene, our friendship was cordial throughout the period. My impression of him is that he was a very kind, thoughtful man, and extremely moral and ethical, quite religious—at least he always made a point of attending mass on Sunday morning.'

The success of *The Glenn Miller Story* led Hollywood to make *The Benny Goodman Story* (1955) in which Gene also appeared, ending the movie with a rousing performance of *Sing, Sing, Sing* at a Hollywood version of the Carnegie Hall concert.

In the late 1950s, Norman Granz recorded Gene with a big band featuring Roy Eldridge and Anita O'Day. All the old hits were revived with some success and a year or so later another album featured the Gerry Mulligan arrangements but there was clearly no marketplace for a permanent big band. The small group tours, inside and outside JATP, continued with visits to Britain (he appeared at the Odeon, Glasgow, in May 1959) and other European venues.

In an attempt to cash in on the success of the movies about Glenn Miller and Benny Goodman, a bio-pic about Gene was prepared. Starring Sal Mineo as Gene and with Anita O'Day appearing as herself, drummer Shelly Manne playing the role of Dave Tough and, thanks to contractual problems, no one playing the part of Benny Goodman, the film proved to be a thoroughgoing embarrassment. By using as its pivot the drugs bust and Gene's early flirtation with a career in the church, the movie failed to capture any of the excitement of Gene's early career, while the absence of a Benny-figure made it impossible to depict his glory days. The only part of the film *The Gene Krupa Story* (1959) (also titled *Drum Crazy*) that had any merit was the soundtrack as Gene played drums for the star to mime to.

Dave Frishberg recalls seeing the movie during the time he was with Gene and in particular 'The scene where the Krupa character drops his sticks during the big solo, and the audience realises that he's "back on the stuff". I remember at least a couple of occasions in real life when Gene dropped a stick, and people in the audience began whispering among themselves and pointing at Gene.'

In 1959 Gene married again. His wife, Patricia Bowler, was some twenty-five years his junior (and once again outside of music). For a while his domestic life appeared as settled as his career. As Bobby Scott recounts, Gene's greatest private sorrow was his inability to father a child. His drugs conviction had made adoption difficult but with the help of church officials, who were more aware of the real man, he and Patricia were able to adopt two children, Marygrace and Gene Michael. The boy was handicapped and Gene devoted much of his time aiding a school for retarded children in Westchester County which Gene Michael attended.

Gene's health was beginning to be suspect. His back gave him trouble, a bad problem for anyone and especially so for a drummer whose posture is to some extent controlled by the needs of his playing. In Gene's case, the physically dramatic

Hollywood's version of the Tommy Dorsey band with Sal Mineo miming to Gene's drumming up front while Shelly Manne impersonates Dave Tough at the back.

COLUMBIA PICTURES presents SAL MINEO (as Gene Krupa) · SUSAN KOHNER · JAMES DARREN
In "DRUM CRAZY —THE GENE KRUPA STORY" "A" with SUSAN OLIVER · RED NICHOLS as Himself · BOBBY TROUP as Tommy Dorsey
ANITA O'DAY as Herself · SHELLEY MANNE as Davey Tough · BUDDY LESTER as Himself   Drums Recorded by Gene Krupa
Written by ORIN JANNINGS, Associate Producer   Directed by DON WEIS   Produced by PHILIP A. WAXMAN   A PHILIP A. WAXMAN PRODUCTION

nature of his performance made matters worse. Then, in 1960, he suffered a heart attact. While not critical, the attack forcibly retired him for several months but as soon as he was able he returned to work. In March 1961 he was at New York's Basin St East with Anita O'Day. *Variety* reported: 'His major moment comes when his colleagues on the bandstand desert same to give [him] an exclusive on the spotlight for a lengthy and showmanly session.'

The Quartet's personnel continued to change with Charlie Ventura returning for a while and pianists Dave Frishberg and John Bunch taking their turn. The gruelling JATP tours were abandoned but were replaced by the first of what would be many happy reunions of the Benny Goodman Quartet. One of the first of these benefited the Wiltwyck School for handicapped children.

Not that Benny's presence was an automatic cause for joy.

Gene juggling with left: *Flip Phillips and* right: *Teddy Napoleon.*

JATP tours brought him to England where he met fans and British jazzmen such as John Dankworth and Alan Ganley.

During the early 1960s Gene's Quartet regularly played the Metropole in New York. One evening in 1962 lives vividly in the memory of pianist Dave Frishberg and conveys the ambivalence with which Gene regarded his old boss: 'We were on the bandstand, just having finished an hour and fifteen minute set, when Benny walked in and the place went crazy. I looked at Gene and his face was white. He says, "It's the King of Swing, and he's got his horn. I don't believe this. Here he comes." So Benny walked up on the stand and began to try out reeds. He stared off into space and tootled and fluttered up and down the scale. This went on for long minutes. Meanwhile Jack Waldorf, the club manager, had herded dozens—hundreds—of passersby into the club, and he had them chanting "Benny! Benny!" Some were hollering out years—like "1936!" The camera girl, standing down by the bar, snapped a picture, and hurried downstairs to make the prints, promising autographs

113

of Goodman and Krupa. Benny was finally ready. He said, "Brushes, Gene." Gene obediently picked up the brushes and flashed a big smile, but I could see he was in a cold fury. Then Benny turned to me and said "*Sweet Lorraine* in G. Give me a little introduction." I complied, and Benny entered in F. He waved me out and continued without piano accompaniment.'

From this unpromising start they played for about an hour. By this time, the camera girl had gone into a second printing. Then, abruptly, Goodman packed up his horn and descended, demanding safe escort through the crowd, and he was gone into the night without signing one picture.

By now, Dave continues, Gene 'was drenched with two shows' worth of perspiration, but he sat patiently on the steps of the bandstand and signed dozens of photos . . . writing personal notes on each one . . . asking each customer, "Who shall I inscribe this to?" Later, in the dressing room, he said to us, "I was glad to sign this picture. This will be in a lot of homes, believe me. Did you get a load of this?" We inspected the picture then, and there was Benny with his clarinet in his mouth, perched on a stool with his legs spread wide. His fly was wide open. "Buttons!" said Gene. "Buttons! That suit's probably from about 1940." '

The touring of Gene's quartet continued through the 1960s with visits to Japan, Mexico and South America and, briefly in 1963, a big band date at Disneyland. There were also TV

Right: *Teddy Wilson, pianist with the BG4, with another giant of jazz piano, Earl Hines.*

Sal Mineo practising for the role of Gene Krupa in the 1959 movie Drum Crazy *while Gene lays down the soundtrack.*

shows, both local and national and very soon the regimen of reduced working commitments was forgotten. He had settled originally into a routine of eighteen weeks at the Metropole in New York with an additional week at Atlantic City's Steel Pier but gradually his engagement book filled right up again. His health began to suffer until, in October 1967, as he observed to John S. Wilson of *The New York Times*, 'I was working in Cincinnati . . . and I felt too lousy to play. And I was sure I sounded lousy. So I decided to go home.'

In 1968 his marriage to Patricia ended. Although he continued to see them he missed the former closeness of his two adopted children. 'What the hell did I go and do?' he said to Bobby Scott.

His professional life revived and he continued making occasional appearances, especially with the Benny Goodman Quartet. There was also a gathering of old friends to celebrate the thirtieth anniversary of the Carnegie Hall concert. And he began a round of lectures to organizations concerned with drug addiction among young people. The parents went along, too,

and as one mother remarked following one such lecture, 'He was to my generation what the Beatles are to my children's.'

Gene's use of his reputation as a means of discouraging youngsters from experimenting with drugs is especially commendable when the long-lasting association of his name with drug-taking is considered. As Dave Frishberg recalls, 'Gene . . . never smoked dope . . . and I understood . . . that he couldn't afford to be compromised in any way. He intimated that the police—especially in the small towns—would like nothing better than to bust Gene Krupa and get some local notoriety . . . I don't even remember seeing Gene take so much as a drink while we were on the job. He was always sharp and alert and ready to perform.'

Given the reality of Gene's lifestyle, the constant association of his name with drug-taking cannot have been other than a permanent thorn in his flesh. Yet he persisted with his lecturing, thus turning an unfair if unspoken criticism into a means of doing good.

His long association with the Slingerland Drum Company

Some of the soundtrack orchestra for Drum Crazy. *Left to right: Clyde Hurley, Jess Stacy, Murray McEachern, Barney Kessell, unknown, Ray Triscari, George Roberts, Joe Triscari, unknown, Benny Carter and Shelley Manne.*

continued and he travelled on their behalf to Frankfurt for a music Trade Fair. (He had never exploited his relationship with the company, persistently refusing their offers to replace his equipment more frequently.)

As the 1970s began he returned to club engagements and in June, 1970, appeared at Plaza 9 where John S. Wilson found 'His featured solos involve more crafty showmanship than the wild abandon of his early days.' As Gene remarked to the reporter, 'I don't have the reflexes that I used to.' His health was still uncertain, however, and late in the year he entered hospital for a laminectomy (an operation designed to alleviate problems associated with the spinal column).

In 1971 Gene was reunited with an old friend from his early days in Chicago when he and Eddie Condon played a date at the New School in New York. With Wild Bill Davison on cornet; Kenny Davern, clarinet; Dick Wellstood, piano; they played for an audience of students. Eddie, laconic as ever, introduced Gene as 'some imposter named Krupa' and quite clearly everyone concerned had a fine and happy time. The concert was recorded by the school's Audio Engineering Class and was later released on an album which provided the final formal record session for both Gene and Eddie. It was forty-four years since they had played together on their first recording date. Dick Wellstood remembers Kenny Davern walking over to put his hand on Gene's arm. 'I just felt I wanted to touch him,' he said. Some years later, Kenny recalled the New School session and remarked of Gene, 'He was a very nice man, a very gentle man, and he played like a demon.'

1972 saw sessions all over New York and surrounding areas. A midnight jam session at Radio City found Gene in company with Roy Eldridge, Benny Carter and others. The reporter for *The New York Times* was not impressed. Referring to Gene as an 'old gladiator of the drums' he remarked that the drummer 'dashed buoyantly on stage and proceeded to hammer away in a style that would have been more appropriate for a Blaze Starr strip show than for the backing of some of the finest jazz players in the world'. But, as he conceded, 'Gene's flair and showmanship sustained him and every tasteless clang of the cymbal was met with shouts of approval from the overflow audience.'

In October Gene appeared at Brandy's II, a rock club, where the audience, young and old, received him enthusiastically. He worked at the Newport in New York Festival and also, late in the year, appeared on TV in an All Star Swing Festival held at the Lincoln Centre. Despite sharing the occasion with the

Throughout his life, and especially as he grew older, Gene's religion was a significant factor. Here he talks with 'jazz priest' Father Norman O'Connor.

orchestras of Duke Ellington and Count Basie, Dave Brubeck and Ella Fitzgerald, the Benny Goodman Quartet (plus a bass player) were quite the best thing in the show. They enjoyed themselves, communicated their pleasure to the audience, and swung mightily.

Early in 1973 his home in Yonkers was badly damaged by fire and all the memorabilia he had accumulated over the years was lost. In the summer, his health clearly failing rapidly, he attended a gathering in Central Park where he was presented with a commemorative plaque signed by many of the leading drummers in jazz.

On 30 June came the Carnegie Hall concert that the Benny Goodman Quartet were obliged to rehearse to ensure that Gene would have the strength. At the concert, the group (rounded out with bass player Slam Stewart) showed no signs of advancing age and Gene's playing had lost none of its dash.

A few days later the Quartet appeared at the Singer Bowl as part of a concert celebrating the renaming of the venue as the Louis Armstrong Stadium. Another session at Ravinia on 15 July and a further one on 18 August at Saratoga Springs brought Gene Krupa's playing career to a close.

The death of Gene's old sidekick, Eddie Condon, brought great sadness and sharp awareness that his own time was fast running out. Towards the end, Eddie, reduced to drinking milk, played host to old friends including Bill Esposito who wrote movingly of his visits in *Jazz Journal* (October 1973). Eddie spoke to Esposito 'of death and he spoke of it without fear. "I went to Gene Krupa's home up in Yonkers a few years back," he said, "when Gene's first wife died. I recall telling him, Krauper—I always called him that and he always called me 'Slick'—Krauper, I guess I'll go to your funeral or you'll go to mine." '

In the event it was Gene who went to Eddie's funeral and was among a number of old friends who spoke. 'I believe in a life hereafter because, Slick, I want to do it all again.'

On the morning of 16 October 1973, Gene Krupa died in bed. He was sixty-four.

The following day there was a wake at Maloney's Funeral Home in Yonkers and, after a Mass on 18 October at St Denis's, his body was flown to Chicago for interment in the Krupa family plot at Holy Cross Cemetery in Calumet City, Illinois.

Newspaper obituaries were generous in their space and praise, although many were typically astray in their facts and dates. Not surprisingly, most mentioned Gene's long-ago involvement with drugs, overstressing the significance of the affair. Also, with some measure of justification, his physical appearance featured prominently, as did his performance with Benny Goodman at Carnegie Hall in 1938 (although several writers placed the event in the wrong year). A few notable exceptions to the contrary, the obituaries were generally lacking in understanding.

Harriet Choice, Chicago *Tribune*: 'Known for his contribution to the Chicago style of jazz, Krupa later went on to achieve fame for his dazzling showmanship and relentless beat. His playing on *Sing, Sing, Sing,* recorded at Carnegie Hall with Benny Goodman in 1937 [sic], still stands as a monument in drum history. There is hardly a drummer today who, in some way, does not owe something to Gene Krupa.'

Jean R. Hailey, *The Washington Post*: 'It was at Carnegie Hall in 1937 [sic] that the quartet [sic] introduced *Sing, Sing, Sing,* a number that featured Mr Krupa on the drums and brought him world fame. The recording of it blared for years from juke boxes across the country. Mr Krupa, whose hands moved so swiftly that cameras had to be speeded up to record the action, was the idol of bobby-soxers, not only because of his rhythm that sent young people into gyrations but also because of his handsome face. As his tempo increased, the black wavy hair fell into his eyes, his head twisted from side to side, his jaw worked at a rapid pace on the chewing gum that seemed an integral part of him. The audience not only heard the music of Gene Krupa. It saw it.'

John S. Wilson (who reported extensively and knowledgeably on Gene's live performances throughout his later years), *The New York Times*: 'As a young man with the Goodman band, Mr Krupa was lean, wiry and handsome. He hunched over his drums, chewing gum in vigorous tempo with the beat, a dangling lock of black hair waving back and forth in front of his eyes, which filled with an almost fiendish zest as he flailed away at his snare drum, tom-toms and cymbals. Suddenly he would rear back, holding both arms in the air as he pounded his bass drum with a foot pedal. And then, perspiration dripping from him like a tropical rainfall, his arms and drumsticks became a blur of motion as he built his solo to a crashing climax.'

George Frazier (another knowledgeable and sympathetic writer), Boston *Globe*, also recalled Carnegie Hall: 'The mounting frenzy of *Sing, Sing, Sing,* with drums like a machine gun battery at Chateau-Thierry. The moment immediately after the finale when the world's greatest tympanist, Sol Goodman, with whom Krupa was studying, burst arms outstretched into the dressing room and embraced his pupil. "You did it! You did it!" he said, saying it all. All that followed after Carnegie must have been a little anticlimactic for Krupa. But what he had had in the good time was enough to last into the fullness of a man's years. He had helped create a new culture, and Zildjian, the cymbal maker, and Slingerland Drums should have been much, much obliged.' After observing that along with Eddie Condon, Gene had been eclipsed by the Rock Era, Frazier ended: 'There was a time, though, when Krupa brought us the gift of excitement, and don't ever forget it either.'

CHAPTER 6

THE LAST ROUND-UP

'Great, Man.'   Buddy Rich

So many changes have occurred in jazz drumming in the years since bebop hit the scene that today's ears find the sometimes staid and rock-like performances of the earlier drummers quite alien.

More astute listeners are aware of the continuity in jazz which binds the music of today to its formative years. The drummers, too, have their links even if the differences between, say, Elvin Jones and Baby Dodds are countless. Even the ability to swing no longer appears a necessity and when a matchless and idiosyncratic practitioner like the ageless Art Blakey declares that above all else he swings, some might argue that his definition of the term is aeons away from Jo Jones.

Yet, for all their dissimilarities, there are links that bind them all. Remove a major link in the chain, like Jo Jones or Kenny Clarke or Max Roach, and the importance of the line can be seen clearly. It would be too much to claim for Gene Krupa that he was a significant link. He did not reshape the fundamentals of jazz drumming. He was, instead, one of a group of drummers who helped move the art several steps beyond the stage it had reached in the hands of the New Orleanians (others included Dave Tough, Chick Webb, Sid Catlett and Buddy Rich) without, curiously enough, being able to make the greater advances signposted by Jones. By the time of Clarke and Roach and their kind, they had become much too set in their ways (Webb had died, while Tough was fast approaching the end of his tragically short life) and either unwilling to learn the new language, or simply incapable of doing so. Those who did learn this new state of the art: Blakey, Philly Joe Jones, Art Taylor,

Mighty drummers:
Gene, Buddy Rich and
Max Roach.

Roy Haynes, Elvin Jones among them, took a route that Krupa
and his kind could never hope to follow.

Not all jazz drummers went the beboppers way, of course.
Others stayed within a stylistic framework that is more readily
identifiable as being from the same roots as Krupa and his
generation. The late Shelly Manne is one (he played the role
of Dave Tough in *The Gene Krupa Story*); another is Louis
Bellson who won a Gene Krupa amateur drummers' contest
in the early 1940s. And there are countless drummers gracing
the jazz scene of the late 1980s in whose style (amidst much
that is far more advanced) can be heard elements well within
Krupa's compass: Frank Capp, Mel Lewis, Jake Hanna, Don
Lamond.

While none of these men might have consciously modelled
himself on Krupa and his peers in their early years, it is difficult
to imagine any drummer working in those areas of jazz outside
bebop and the fusions who have not been influenced in some
way. Perhaps that influence is unconscious or indirect, but it
is there.

Such assertions are, of course, impossible to substantiate
other than by urging a thorough and lengthy exercise of

listening to their work and tracing stylistic influences. It is similarly impossible to estimate how many young men took up drumming as a result of seeing and hearing Gene.

There are, however, a few clues. Drummer Roy Porter, who worked with Charlie Parker, spoke at length to Mark Gardner for *Jazz and Blues*. 'I think Gene Krupa was the influence that started a lot of youngsters playing. He made me start digging drums . . . I liked the way he was playing solos . . . he made the public aware of drum solos.'

Butch Miles, in conversation with Eddie Cook of *Jazz Journal International*, recalls that Gene was his first favourite. 'When I was back in high school, I used to do an impression of him.'

Roy Haynes considered him 'a wonderful person and a great master of his instrument'.

Ultimately, however, it was in a non-musical sense that Gene Krupa most affected the drummers of his day and those who came afterwards. He changed perceptions of the drummer in jazz, made him an accepted soloist and, in his own words, 'a high-priced guy'. Unfortunately, the inspiration felt by many young men was limited to the flash and spectacle of his live performance rather than what he was actually playing. He appealed to Buddy Rich for his showmanship, yet listening to his playing on record there is remarkably little aural evidence of flamboyance.

If the listener approaches a Krupa recording without a mental image of his visual presence (an admittedly difficult task because there is a 'once seen, never forgotten' quality about him) then what emerges is a remarkable solidity of performance. Even that most famous of his recordings, *Sing, Sing, Sing,* is a controlled and, by latterday standards, sedate exercise.

This distinction between sight and sound is something which has been overlooked by those drummers who merely copied the visual image. It is also overlooked by many critics whose comments, even fifteen years after his death, are clearly controlled by memories of how he looked on-stage or, more often than not, in movies. Certainly, Gene's stage presentation (which the obituary writers made much of) was excessive while his movie appearances took matters a regrettable stage further. (Louis Armstrong once appeared in a film wearing an animal skin, a vulgar excess for which the moviemakers were rightly blamed. Krupa's excesses are all blamed on him.)

Of course, some of those excesses were real and criticism of them justified. Even the (accurate) claim that this is what audiences wanted is a feeble excuse. But, importantly, Krupa's habits: the gum-chewing, the facial grimaces, the bodily contortions, the whole-heartedness with which he threw himself into sweating, grunting performances, were not something he put on just for public appearances. Those who saw him in rehearsal confirm that he always behaved in the same way. Perhaps everything was exaggerated on-stage, but only the dramatic lighting of the bandstand or the movie set were purely theatrical. Every time he played he committed himself totally, especially in a physical sense, to the performance.

Setting aside visual images and considering only his music, Gene Krupa showed better than many other examples in the world of jazz just how important are early influences of environment. From the New Orleans master drummers who worked in Chicago in the 1920s he took the essence of good timekeeping and a rock-steady beat. From the city's breezy, extrovert character he took his dynamism and wrapped it in the often noisy enthusiasm of his fellow Chicagoans. From the New York scene he took the more sophisticated elements of performance, and the showbiz glitter of extrovert drummers like Catlett and Webb.

Then there was his commercialism, which doubtless brought upon him the wrath of those who, rightly, deplore the commercialization of jazz. As has been shown here, the heady atmosphere of the birth of the Swing Era was inextricably tangled with a period of acute economic depression. With Krupa, as with Benny Goodman and many others, it is difficult to mount a wholly supportable critique for 'selling out'. For any man, musician or not, especially if he has even the slightest trace of sensitivity, to see and know poverty and hard times must effect a change of attitude. In Gene Krupa's case he chose, consciously or not, to capitalize upon his popularity and ensure that he was never poor again.

Gene Krupa, then, was a creature of his times, of his environment. In the course of his career he also became a symbol of the times through which he lived. Long after the Swing Era ended he remains one of its most durable images.

However, in approaching an examination of his long recording career it is necessary for those who saw Gene Krupa on-stage or on film to try to place themselves in the mental shoes of the younger generation of listeners who have no such preconceptions. Music is, after all, an aural art and the eyes have no role to play.

CHAPTER 7

STOP! THE RED LIGHT'S ON
THE RECORD SESSIONS

'You know, I feel awfully good about these things.'
Gene Krupa

Compiling a discography for any prolific artist is a specialized, thankless and ultimately self-defeating task, compounded equally of scholarship and antiquarianism. New issues and reissues of the recordings of major jazz artists appear almost daily—only to be inexplicably withdrawn, amended or deleted within an equally short time. Again, in an age of 'budget' and 'nice price' (as well as imported) records and cassettes, old albums appear in partially or totally new guises—often with new titles and curiously lacking in details of recording dates and personnel. For these reasons, the recordings listed in this discographical essay are identified by title wherever possible and last known label and number. Many of the records cited, especially those recorded under Gene's own name, will be available only from specialist jazz record shops and even then, perhaps, in the second-hand rack.

Any reader seeking additional information on recording sessions including full personnel details is directed to the discography of recordings made under Gene's name between 1935 and 1972: *Gene Krupa and His Orchestra* edited by George I. Hall and published in June 1975 by Jazz Discographies Unlimited, Laurel, Maryland.

*   *   *   *

Gene Krupa's recording career began in 1927 with the band named the McKenzie and Condon Chicagoans. While decidedly rough around the edges, these sides present a lively impression of the youthful enthusiasm of McPartland, Teschemacher,

Freeman, Sullivan, Lannigan, Condon and Krupa. The four tunes recorded by this band, *Sugar, China Boy, Nobody's Sweetheart* and *Liza*, together with *Oh Baby* and *Indiana*, which were recorded by Tesch, Sullivan, Eddie and Gene during their New York scuffle in the summer of 1928, can be heard on 'That Toddlin' Town—Chicago: 1926-28' (Parlophone PMC 7072). The two quartet titles are interesting for the excitement generated by an admittedly undisciplined Krupa. Despite the fuss over the records when they were first released, today's listener will observe that Gene's playing is felt rather than heard. This comment applies even when one tune, *Nobody's Sweetheart*, is heard in the marvellously restored sound quality of Robert Parker's digitally remastered series of albums: 'Jazz Classics in Digital Stereo: Vol. 2 Chicago' (BBC REB 589). Various titles recorded during 1928 by the Chicago Rhythm Kings, Frank Teschemacher's Chicagoans and Wingy Manone and his Club Royale Orchestra are on 'Chicago Jazz Volume 1: Frank Teschemacher' (Classic Jazz Masters CJM 31). On some of these performances the drumming style of Gene Krupa is not yet distinctive but is very different from that of Dave Tough.

Readers may be interested to pursue a line of thought suggested by Theodore Dennis Brown in his absorbing and superbly researched (unpublished) doctoral thesis, *A History and Analysis of Jazz Drumming to 1942*, one complete chapter of which is devoted to Gene's work. In this, the writer draws technical parallels between Gene's early style and that of drummers Bob Conselman and the virtually unknown Paul Kettler.

One particular tune from this period and included on CJM 31, *There'll Be Some Changes Made* (by the Rhythm Kings), is a fine example of Gene's urgent, yet supportive drumming style already beyond the embryo stage.

Some of the Red Nichols sides recorded in New York in April 1929 appear on Affinity AFS 1018 and already improvements can be heard in Gene's playing. Benny Goodman is present on these same tracks. Some of Gene's 1930 New York work (with the Irving Mills Hotsy Totsy Gang) appear on this same album which thus gives an interesting cross-section of the white New York jazz scene of the period. Several titles also appear on 'Benny Goodman: the Formative Years (1927-1934)' (Decca RAL 508) and on Vocalion VLP 2.

In November 1929 Gene was present on a recording date which quickly passed into legend when Coleman Hawkins played with the Mound City Blue Blowers. *Hello Lola*, a lively but tight piece, and the molten majesty of *One Hour* are undeniable jazz classics but it would be absurd to pretend that

Gene's contribution on this date is of any particular significance. Similarly, his later appearance (in 1933) on Billie Holiday's first recording date is of interest for reasons that have nothing to do with his drumming.

A Hoagy Carmichael session from May 1930 features Bix Beiderbecke of whom Whitney Balliett (no admirer of Krupa) wrote, 'Whenever Krupa worked behind him, [his] rhythmic stiffness disappeared, and he gained some of the flow of his Negro colleagues.' *Rockin' Chair* and *Barnacle Bill the Sailor* were cut on this date and appear on several albums, among them RCA International INTS 5181 and one of RCA's Jazz Tribune series of double albums, 'The Indispensable Bix Beiderbecke (1924-1930)' (RCA NL 89572).

Although Gene had already appeared on record with Benny Goodman, his first session under Benny's name can be heard on the odd track on 'Benny Goodman: the Early Years Volume 2, 1931-1933' (Sunbeam SB 138) which also includes an excellent Charleston Chasers set from 1931 with Jack Teagarden playing and singing *Basin Street Blues* and *Beale Street Blues*. (The second title is also on Decca RAL 508.) Sunbeam SB 138 also features the 1933 Goodman sessions with Teagarden and fine performances of *I Gotta Right to Sing the Blues* (also on the Decca Album), *Ain't-Cha Glad?*, *Dr Heckle and Mr Jibe* and *Texas Tea Party*. On all these dates Gene lends solid and unobtrusive support.

Benny Goodman's light was hidden behind the bushel known as 'Bill Dodge and his Orchestra' in February and March 1934. This band, which included the excellent Shirley Clay, trumpet, on most titles, and Mannie Klein, trumpet and Jack Jenny, trombone, on others, appears on Hot 'n' Sweet HOL 6427. The transient nature of the band is reflected in some of the ensemble passages but it is already clear from this why Benny was beginning to think of using Gene on a permanent basis.

Benny's Music Hall band of 1934 (without Gene) can be heard on the Decca album and on 'Breakfast Ball' (Saville SVL 172) and offers interesting aural evidence of the difference made by Gene's arrival on a permanent basis. He provided the spark needed, as can be heard on the majority of the tracks on Sunbeam SB 100, SB 104, and SB 150, all of which are taken from radio broadcasts up to 13 April 1934.

Recording under the name 'The Rhythm Makers' a good series of sessions from around 6 June 1935 finds the band settling down well (Sunbeam SB 101, SB 102, SB 103).

The drummer employed Benny for a session in November 1935, when Gene Krupa and his Chicagoans recorded four titles:

The Last Round-Up, Jazz Me Blues, Three Little Words and an excellent *Blues of Israel* featuring bass player Israel Crosby. In a letter to Wellington Holiday written a little over a year later, Gene remarked that Crosby was 'still on the "up and coming" list. It remains to be seen just how far he will go!' In 1935, Crosby was only sixteen years old and this session was his recording debut. As it turned out, despite this auspicious beginning, his later career was something of a disappointment despite working with Teddy Wilson, Goodman, and Gene during the 1950s and with George Shearing in the 1960s. He died in 1962, aged forty-three. The Gene Krupa Chicagoans sessions can be heard on 'Swingin' With Krupa' (RCA Camden 340) while the first two titles are on 'King of Swing' (Music for Pleasure MFP 1069) which also has Jess Stacy's *Barrelhouse* recorded by Stacy, Crosby and Gene.

The Goodman band's growing popularity led to a series of formal studio sessions under a new contract with RCA Victor. These sessions are generally available in the RCA Jazz Tribune

series, 'The Indispensable Benny Goodman'. The sessions recorded between 25 June 1935 and 5 November 1936 can be heard on 'Birth of a Big Band Volumes 1/2 (1935-1936)' (RCA NL 89755). Good performances of Fletcher Henderson's arrangements of *Blue Skies, Sometimes I'm Happy, When Buddha Smiles, Christopher Columbus* (later to evolve into *Sing, Sing, Sing*), *Down South Camp Meeting* feature together with arrangements from Jimmy Mundy (*Madhouse* and *Bugle Call Rag* among them). This particular album also includes four tracks by Gene Krupa's Swing Band. One is a driving *I Hope Gabriel Likes My Music* with Krupa's drumming underpinning a fiery Roy Eldridge, trumpet; and the effortlessly swinging Chu Berry, tenor saxophone. Benny; Jess Stacy, piano; Allan Reuss, guitar; and Crosby, round out a fine and often overlooked small band, regrettably gathered together for only this one date. The other titles are *Mutiny in the Parlour, I'm Gonna Clap My Hands* (both with vocals by Helen Ward) and a fast and furious *Swing Is Here*.

One of the Goodman band's live broadcasts from the breakthrough engagement at the Palomar Ballroom in Los Angeles provides three tracks on 'BG on the Air—1935-1936' (Sunbeam SB 105) while the extended engagement at Chicago's Congress Hotel can be heard on several Sunbeam albums: SB 128, SB 129, SB 130, SB 132. Later broadcasts, from 1937, mostly transmitted from the 'Madhattan Room' during a New York hotel stint appear on several more Sunbeam albums, including the consecutive sequence numbered SB 116 to SB 126 inclusive.

Contrasting the band in its studio and live recordings is interesting (as it often is with jazz musicians). The studio recordings are generally much stiffer, perhaps reflecting Benny the disciplinarian. Gene's work on most tracks, especially the live broadcasts, give some aural evidence of the reason for his popular appeal. He is much more assertive and is certainly louder than his counterparts. (Contrast, for example, the earlier Fletcher Henderson Orchestra's versions of arrangements also recorded by Benny.) A further example of the band in the recording studios can be heard on the RCA 'Indispensable Benny Goodman' series, 'Volume 3/4 (1936-1937)' (NL 89756), while the more freewheeling music of the live dates can be heard on the misleadingly titled '1937-38 Jazz Concert No. 2' (CBS 54129/30).

The Benny Goodman Trio and Quartet feature on 'Benny Goodman: the Complete Small Combinations Volumes 1/2 (1935-1937)' and 'Volumes 3/4 (1937-1939)' (RCA NL 89753 and

NL 89754). The elegance of Teddy Wilson's piano playing and his superb interplay with Benny are well supported by Gene in restrained mood. Alun Morgan, writing in *Jazz and Blues* in 1971, remarked of Krupa in this context that at the time he 'must have been one of the most flexible and accomplished drummers in jazz. He could scale down his normal attack, when he was punching home the accents behind a full ensemble, to the level of the most intimate of jazz trios, urging Benny and Teddy Wilson along with the minimum of volume.' Theodore Dennis Brown argues most persuasively that the finest work of Gene's career was recorded at this time and in this setting. With Lionel Hampton's arrival, the mood changed. There could still be elegance but now it had a more sonorous texture thanks to Lionel's vibraphone while on the up-tempo numbers Gene responded to Lionel's dynamism.

For the most part Gene's solos are spare and thoughtfully constructed. On *Who?*, recorded on 13 July 1935, his brushwork in his solo is especially fine. Gene's own favourite recording of this series, the one on which he felt he produced his best recorded work, is the version of *Runnin' Wild* from 3 February 1937. On this tune (which, with *Who?*, appears on RCA NL 89753) the tempo is set by Gene (using brushes which he favoured for his small group work and of which he became a master of what has latterly become a dying art). His steady beat is applied with subtle differences behind his companions as first Teddy, then Benny, finally Lionel, take their solos. In the closing ensemble he urges his companions along until the final few bars when he lays out.

Among the criticisms levelled at Krupa is an inability to maintain steady tempi. While it would be claiming too much to suggest he never rushed the beat, there is very little evidence of this characteristic in his recordings. With Goodman the only notable instance is the Carnegie Hall concert.

Thanks to the foresight (or plain good luck) of Albert Marks, who recorded the concert on 16 January 1938, this marvellous occasion has become one of the best-selling records in the history of jazz. From the opening of *Don't Be That Way* the band sounds understandably overawed but a blast from Gene's drums brings everyone into line and marginally adjusts the tempo (and draws the first cheer of the night from the crowd). A short 'history of jazz' sequence gives way to more numbers from the band and a delightful (and often overlooked) *Blue Reverie* by Benny, Gene, Allan Reuss and Jess Stacy (giving a foretaste of what was to come) from the Goodman band with guests Cootie Williams, trumpet; Johnny Hodges, alto saxophone; and Harry Carney, baritone saxophone; from Duke Ellington's orchestra.

The jam session on *Honeysuckle Rose* is deservedly highly regarded, featuring as it does a contingent from the Basie band. This included three-fourths of the greatest rhythm section of the era, with only Jo Jones dropping out to be replaced by Gene. The full personnel for this part of the show is: Harry James and Buck Clayton, trumpets; Vernon Brown, trombone; Lester Young, tenor saxophone; Benny, Hodges, Carney; Count Basie, piano; Freddie Green, guitar; Walter Page, bass; and Gene.

Then it was the turn of the Trio and Quartet and it is here that the tempi begin to go awry. The up-tempo numbers become real flag-wavers but at least served to raise the evening's temperature. After more big band numbers and a return by the small groups, it was time for the finale. Gene's tom-tomming introduction to *Sing, Sing, Sing* was met with more whistles and yells. This *tour-de-force* by Gene is somewhat overshadowed by Jess Stacy's remarkable piano solo, but was a perfect way to end the evening. (In fact, and possibly unwisely, the band played on, performing two encores which prove to be somewhat anticlimactic.)

The 'Carnegie Hall Concert' (except for the second tune of the night and the first of the two encores) is available on CBS 54127/28, or on CBS 66202. (A CBS boxed set of four records, CBS 66420, comprises the Carnegie Hall concert and the falsely named Jazz Concert No. 2 from CBS 54129/30.) The two tunes omitted from the CBS records due to imperfect sound, *Sometimes I'm Happy* and *If Dreams Come True*, can be heard on Sunbeam SB 127.

Gene's first band made its first records on 14 and 15 April 1938 (the band's first live appearance was 16 April). Despite the evidence of heavy orientation towards drum solos in public performances, little that appears on the commercial recordings suggests this. Indeed, with only occasional exceptions, the bulk of this band's recorded output was ordinary. The compilation of Krupa big band tracks released on 'Drummin' Man' (CBS BPG 62289, BPG 62290) includes, from 1938, Gene's first theme song, *Apurksody,* plus *Rhythm Jam* and *Tutti Frutti*, which features vocalist Leo Watson; from 1939, *Drummin' Man*, the band's first hit which features vocalist Irene Daye, *Quiet and Roll 'Em* and, from 1940 and 1941, an effective cover version of Erskine Hawkin's *Tuxedo Junction* and *Drum Boogie* which became another big seller. Three tunes from Gene's appearance in the movie *Some Like It Hot* can be found on 'Film Tracks of Gene Krupa and Buddy Rich' (Joyce 3002) which suffers from poor sound transfer. Even worse sound quality affects Fanfare

10-110 but does allow comparison between the studio recordings and live performances of such tunes as the popular *Wire Brush Stomp* and *Murdy Purdy*. Good studio recordings of *Jungle Madness* and *Blue Rhythm Fantasy* are on Sounds of Swing LP-114 which generally offers tunes usually left off other compilations. (The 'Drummin' Man' compilation is enhanced by excellent sleeve notes which take the form of a discussion between George T. Simon and Gene whose delight in hearing these tunes again is very evident: 'I didn't realize that we'd made so many good records.')

The arrival of Anita O'Day and Roy Eldridge lit the missing fire. Anita came into the band first and recorded *Georgia On My Mind* on 12 March 1941 which appears on 'Gene Krupa in Disco Order Volume 11' (Ajax/Ajaz 138). A little heard recording session at the slightly echo-prone Leiderkrantz Hall studio in New York is available on Blue Heaven BH 6-608 which includes some interesting Elton Hill arrangements, *Full Dress Hop, Tunin' Up* and one of Gene's own but infrequent charts, *Siren Serenade*, complete with cop-car howl. The Roy Eldridge classics, *Let Me Off Uptown* (with Anita's famous 'Blow, Roy, blow!' exhortation), a lip-searing *After You've Gone* and, best of all, *Rockin' Chair* are all on Volume 1 of the CBS 'Drummin' Man' album.

Most of the studio recordings from April 1938 up to early 1952 appear on a series of albums on the Ajax label (later renamed Ajaz) under the general title, 'Gene Krupa in Disco Order'. These set out the tunes chronologically and make no allowances for quality of material. This policy, allied to often poor sound quality (the tunes are mainly dubbed from 78s) makes these records of interest more to a specialist Krupa collector than to the more selective purchaser. The Ajax/Ajaz series are numbered 101, 105, 110, 111, 121, 122, 125, 127, 130, 132, 138, 146, 154, 161, 167, 203, 211, 219, 227, 241, 262.

Gene's return to recording after his prison term came with Benny Goodman's band which toured USO camps in 1943. Although suffering from inferior sound quality, 'Benny Goodman: The Forgotten Year—1943' (Swing Treasury 103) affords a fascinating glimpse of Gene at a time of personal crisis. As indicated elsewhere in this book, his response to Benny's offer of this job resulted in some of his best big band playing. On *Seven Come Eleven* (a tune more usually associated with Goodman's Sextet) Gene's drumming is strikingly reminiscent of Chick Webb's on an arrangement which in its interplay between drums and orchestra closely resembles Chick's recording of *Liza*. This album also includes a long version of

Sing, Sing, Sing but although Jess Stacy had also been rehired by Benny there is no repeat of his Carnegie Hall pianistic triumph.

Gene's stint with Tommy Dorsey's band was recorded for V-Disc and the band was also picked up on some airshots. 'Radio Discs of Tommy Dorsey' (Joyce LP 2004) has Gene prominent on several tracks including *Swing High* (which can be contrasted with the better known commercial recording by Dorsey with Buddy Rich on drums) and *Not So Quiet Please* which was usually Buddy's party-piece.

Gene's first appearance with Norman Granz's Jazz at the Philharmonic appears on Melodisc MLP 13-301. Curiously, but presumably for some contractural reason, this session has not been included in Granz's extensive programme of issues of JATP on his own labels. Two tunes are performed: *How High the Moon* and *Oh! Lady Be Good* and both feature Gene in extended solos but his playing is already showing signs of incompatibility with the more modern musicians, particularly trumpet players Howard McGhee and Joe Guy. From the same year, 1945, a New York Town Hall concert has Gene with Charlie Ventura, tenor saxophone and George Walters, piano, taking things very un-seriously. 'Commodore Town Hall Concert—Vol. 2' (London HMC 5002) includes *Stompin' at the Savoy* and *Limehouse Blues*. Gene's Trio studio recordings with Ventura (and Teddy Napoleon, piano) also appear on the 'Drummin' Man' album.

Gene's band 'that swings with strings' appears on 'King Krupa' (Swing Treasury 106) which has excellent performances of *Challenging the Challenger, Blue Lou* and an amiably swinging *King Porter Stomp*.

The 1945 Krupa band can be heard on 'Drummin' Man' with a headlong version of *Lover* and much more relaxed performances of *Boogie Blues* and a cover version of Tommy Dorsey's hit, *Opus 1*. One of the band's best and most popular recordings from this period, *Leave Us Leap*, is also on this album. (Confusion persists with this recording as another drummer was employed by Gene at this time to stand in when he was conducting. The aural evidence of Gene's presence on this tune is unmistakable.) Once again, it is possible to compare the studio sessions with broadcast performances by hearing Hep 16 and Fanfare 34-134, both of which albums draw heavily upon a 31 March 1946 broadcast from Meadowbrook Gardens in Culver City, Los Angeles.

The Gerry Mulligan arrangements and those of George Williams gave the 1947 band a marvellously distinctive sound and also brought more successful recordings, among them *Disc Jockey Jump* and *Gene's Boogie.* Both are on 'Drummin' Man' as are *Calling Dr Gillespie* and *Up and Atom* from the same year. On the same compilation is another bebop-flavoured hit recording, *Lemon Drop,* which comes from 1949. As indicated, at this time Gene often employed a deputy drummer (Louis Zito was one, Joe Dale another) to take his place when he led the band. For the most part, however, he appears to have played on record dates. Although Theodore Dennis Brown agrees with many discographers in saying that Gene does not play on *Leave Us Leap* and *Disc Jockey Jump,* it is clearly Gene's drumming on both these recordings.

Other albums which include tracks by the bands of the mid-1940s are: 'Ace Drummer Man' (Giants of Jazz GOJ 1006) and 'What's This?' (Hep 20).

Gene's 1949 band, with many arrangements by Gerry Mulligan and using material from 'One Night Stand' broadcasts, can be heard on 'Gene Krupa 1944-51: the Transition Years' (Renkcurb 11D-1810). Among the featured soloists are Buddy Wise, tenor saxophone; Don Fagerquist and Roy Eldridge, trumpets; Urbie Green, trombone; and the vocal talents of Dave Lambert and Buddy Stewart.

The 1950 date which produced an album of Fats Waller songs appears on RCA International INTS 1072 and RCA Camden 340 (and is also covered on Ajaz 241). This session is frankly disappointing but is interesting as a near-final act of the Krupa big band story. The RCA albums also include tracks recorded by Gene Krupa's Chicago Jazz Band (in September 1950) featuring Wild Bill Davison, cornet; Edmond Hall, clarinet; and Bobby Soots, an entirely inappropriate singer.

In 1951 Benny Goodman, Teddy Wilson and Gene Krupa were reunited for a concert performance to raise funds for a very sick Fletcher Henderson. After playing some of their old standbys, *Runnin' Wild* among them, the Trio was expanded by one man for each succeeding number until the group became a septet (Buck Clayton, trumpet, was the last to join). Although the occasion was sad, the music was happy and very obviously all the old enthusiasm had not dimmed. 'The Benny Goodman Trio Plays for the Fletcher Henderson Fund' is on Tax m 8041.

Gene's visit to Japan in 1952 with Ventura and Napoleon was recorded and can be heard on 'The World's Greatest Drummer 1952-1961' (Sunbeam SB 225 and also on Ajaz 262) but is notable more for the enthusiasm of performers and audience alike than for feeling. A May 1953 recording date for Norman Granz, together with sessions in September and

November, produced some of Gene's more interesting small band tracks from this period. The first date is by a Sextet featuring Gene with Charlie Shavers, trumpet; Willie Smith, alto saxophone; Teddy Wilson, piano; Steve Jordan, guitar; Israel Crosby, bass. Tunes include *Coronation Hop*, which has mildly boppish overtones on which Gene uses cymbals more than was his custom and thus helps retain something of the idiom of the arrangement. Gene's marked reluctance to use cymbals instead of the more traditional snare drum for his supporting playing consistently sets him apart from most drummers of both his and later eras. When he does make the shift, as here, it is apparent that his failure to use the medium is not related to inability; clearly, he elected to do otherwise. (Not that this should be taken as suggesting he was capable of using cymbals in the manner of the bebop drummers—that is a very different matter.)

The September 1953 date teamed Gene, Shavers and Wilson with Bill Harris, trombone; Ben Webster, tenor saxophone; Herb Ellis, guitar; Ray Brown, bass. A crisp *Midget* is pushed along by Gene in a manner which encourages good solos from Harris and, especially, Webster. The November date replaced Webster with Eddie 'Lockjaw' Davis, Wilson with Teddy Napoleon and dropped Ellis. An up-tempo *Bloozy Woozy* and a swinging *Meddle My Minor* come from this date. Gene's playing (very well-recorded) mixes many of the familiar old licks with some clear attempts to absorb a different style of drumming. Although not entirely successful, the resulting album 'The Exciting Gene Krupa' always holds the attention (Verve MGV 8087 and Metro 2356 010).

JATP sessions from the early 1950s feature Gene with Benny Carter, alto saxophone, and Oscar Peterson, piano, including the 1953 Nichigeki Theatre, Tokyo, concert which produced *Indiana, Stompin' at the Savoy* and others. These appear on a three-record set on Verve 2660-112 and Pablo Live 2620 104.

In 1955, while in Hollywood for the movie *The Benny Goodman Story*, Gene recorded with Teddy Wilson, Lionel Hampton and Red Callender, bass, an excellent set of old Benny Goodman Quartet standards but without Benny. *Avalon, Moonglow, Airmail Special, I Got Rhythm* and others appear on 'Kings of Swing' (Verve 2683 055). Everyone is in fine form and appear not to miss their old boss. The soundtrack album for the movie is of doubtful merit. Although it uses a selection of fine musicians, the performances are a little wooden and are not helped by a rather muddy recording sound (Coral COPS 5162-D/1-2).

Norman Granz reunited Gene with some of his old gang for a 1956 recording session of all the old hits. Anita and Roy were on hand and if the result failed to capture the brilliance of the originals, there was enough of the old magic left to make it an enjoyable occasion (Verve 2317 078).

Another Granz session, this time in 1958, brought together a big band to perform the Gerry Mulligan arrangements of a decade earlier. Once again, it was a very creditable near-miss (Verve 2683 055).

The soundtrack album 'The Gene Krupa Story' for the movie of the same name (Verve MGV 15010) was recorded in 1959. It is very much a mixed bag with Gene in good form but with a somewhat lacklustre band despite the presence in its ranks of Benny Carter and the Candoli brothers. A dixieland-style

The Benny Goodman Trio in full cry: Gene, Teddy and Benny.

band reunited Gene and Red Nichols but most honours go to Anita O'Day for her one appearance on the album, a sensitive reading of *Memories Of You*.

Also in 1959, a performance by the Benny Goodman Quartet (not, strictly speaking, a reunion because Teddy Wilson's place is taken by Jess Stacy), together with some Trio performances with Wilson, from 1961 can be heard on Goodman compilation albums (Festival 246 and Rarities 30).

A 1961 recording date featuring light classical music, *Ritual Fire Dance, Sabre Dance*, the overture from *Poet and Peasant* and the like, was something of a self-indulgence for Gene. If 'Classics in Percussion' (Verve VLP 9005) fails to come off, it is all harmless enough fun.

Gene's drum battles with Buddy Rich get an airing on Verve MGV 8369 (1952) World Record Club T 248 (1955) and Verve 2317 057 (1962), while a similar sort of thing, but this time with Louis Bellson and recorded in 1963, can be found on 'The Mighty Two' (Columbia 33SX1571). Of these, the tracks recorded with Rich in November 1955 are the best. Essentially a JATP unit, but recorded in the studio, this session features Roy Eldridge, Dizzy Gillespie, trumpets; Illinois Jacquet, Flip Phillips, tenor saxophones; Oscar Peterson, piano; and Ray Brown, bass. *Bernie's Tune, I Never Knew* and *Sweethearts On Parade* give just about everyone a chance to blow and the drummers are not as obtrusive as might be feared. For the two remaining tracks, *Buddy's Blues* and *Gene's Blues*, one drummer lays out, affording an interesting opportunity for assessing their differences without the clamour of the joust.

A broadcast from the early 1960s teamed Gene with singer Tony Bennett. While suffering from some mildly embarrassing introductions by the stars, in company with announcer Martin Block, there are some good musical moments (Sunbeam P 509).

1963 saw the first of the reunions of the Benny Goodman Quartet. Although they would make many such appearances together in the next ten years, the four sessions which took place in February and August contributed towards what was to be the only formal studio teaming. On 'Together Again!' (RCA NL 89304) the four perform with considerable vigour (if anything, Benny is slightly overshadowed by his companions) on some old standards, *Seven Come Eleven, I've Found a New Baby, Runnin' Wild* and one or two tunes not usually associated with the group.

Gene's own quartet recorded a number of times during the 1950s and 1960s: Columbia 33CX10118 and 33CX10133, Hall of Fame JG 633, Metro 2356 010. The last formal session was in January and February 1964 when, with Ventura, John Bunch, piano, and Nabil Tobah, bass, a mixed bag of Ellingtonia, popular songs of the day, old standards and a Krupa arrangement of *Come Back to Sorrento* were rounded out with a snappy *Flying Home* (Verve VLP 9072).

Transcriptions of radio and TV broadcasts of various small groups, particularly the Quartet, can also be found. These include a set with Charlie Ventura and Dave Frishberg which was recorded during a week-long engagement at Atlantic City's Steel Pier in August 1962 and released on an album entitled 'Perdido' (Swing House SWH 21).

Although tapes (not commercially available) of broadcasts made as late as June 1973 are to be found, Gene's final recording date came in April 1972 when, with Wild Bill Davison, cornet; Kenny Davern, clarinet; Dick Wellstood, piano; and his old friend Eddie Condon, he visited the New School in New York. The occasion produced some highly enjoyable music. Clearly no one had much inclination towards introspection (although there is, unusually for such a group, an interesting performance of Duke Ellington's *The Mooche*). Most of the numbers (*I Want to Be Happy, Shim Me Sha Wabble, Avalon*) are performed with a gleeful abandon that only hindsight saddens. Within months Eddie and Gene would die but on this night they could have been beating out the old tunes in one of the Chicago speakeasies of their youth. 'Jazz at the New School' (Chiaroscuro CR 110) is a fitting close to Gene Krupa's recording career.

BIBLIOGRAPHY

This bibliography includes books cited in the text and other works which may prove of interest to the reader.

Abel, Alan — *The Confessions of a Hoaxer* (New York: Macmillan, 1970)

Addams, Jane — *Twenty Years at Hull-House* (New York: New American Library, 1961)

Allen, Frederick Lewis — *Only Yesterday: An Informal History of the Nineteen-twenties in America* (London; Pelican, 1938)

Since Yesterday: The Nineteen-thirties in America (New York: Bantam, 1961)

Allsop, Kenneth — *The Bootleggers: The Story of Chicago's Prohibition Era* (London: Hutchinson, 1968 and London: Arrow, 1970)

Anderson, Jervis — *Harlem: The Great Black Way, 1900-1950* (New York: Farrar, Straus & Giroux and London: Orbis, 1982)

Balliett, Whitney — *Dinosaurs in the Morning* (Philadelphia: Lippincott, 1962 and London: Jazz Book Club, 1965)

Improvising (New York: Oxford University Press, 1977)

The Sound of Surprise (New York: Dutton, 1959 and London: Jazz Book Club, 1961)

Barker, Danny — *A Life in Jazz* (London: Macmillan, 1986)

Blesh, Rudi — *Combo: U.S.A. Eight Lives in Jazz* (Philadelphia: Chilton, 1971)

Brown, Theodore Dennis — *A History and Analysis of Jazz Drumming to 1942* Ph.D. thesis, University of Michigan, 1976. Available through Xerox University Microfilms, Ann Arbor, Michigan.

Charters, Samuel B., — *Jazz: A History of the New York*

and Leonard Kunstadt   *Scene* (New York: Doubleday, 1962)

Chilton, John   *Billie's Blues: A Survey of Billie Holiday's Career (1933-1959)* (London: Quartet, 1975)

Jazz (London: Hodder & Stoughton, 1979)

Condon, Eddie, and Thomas Sugrue   *We Called it Music* (New York: Holt, 1947, and London: Peter Davies, 1948)

Condon, Eddie, and Richard Gehman, eds.   *Eddie Condon's Treasury of Jazz* (New York: Dial Press, 1956 and London: Peter Davies, 1957)

Condon, Eddie   *The Eddie Condon Scrapbook of Jazz* (New York: St. Martins, 1973 and London: Hale, 1974)

Dahl, Linda   *Stormy Weather* (New York: Pantheon and London: Quartet, 1984)

Dance, Stanley, ed.   *Jazz Era: The 'Forties* (London: MacGibbon and Kee, 1961)

Erenberg, Lewis A.   *Steppin' Out: New York Nightlife and the Transformation of American Culture, 1890-1930* (Westport, Connecticut: Greenwood Press, 1981)

Farrell, James T.   *Studs Lonigan: A Trilogy* (New York: Vanguard, 1935)

Feather, Leonard   *The Book of Jazz* (New York: Horizon Press, 1957 and London: Jazz Book Club, 1961)

Goodman, Benny, and Irving Kolodin   *The Kingdom of Swing* (New York: Ungar, 1939)

Hadlock, Richard   *Jazz Masters of the Twenties* (New York: Macmillan, 1965)

Hammond, John, and Irving Townsend   *John Hammond on Record* (London: Penguin, 1981)

Hentoff, Nat   *Jazz Is* (New York: Random House, 1976 and London: W. H. Allen, 1978)

Hentoff, Nat, and Albert McCarthy, eds.   *Jazz* (London: Quartet, 1977)

Jones, Maldwyn A.   *Destination America* (London: Weidenfeld & Nicholson, 1976)

Krupa, Gene   'Drums' in *Rhythm*, May 1938

Krupa, Gene, and Leonard Bernstein
'Jazz Forum: Has Jazz Influenced the Symphony?' in *Esquire*, February 1947

Mayer, Harold M. and Richard C. Wade
Chicago: Growth of a Metropolis (Chicago: University of Chicago Press, 1973)

Mezzrow, Mezz and Bernard Wolfe
Really the Blues (New York: Random House, 1946)

Miller, Paul Eduard, ed.
Esquire's Book of Jazz (New York: Barnes and London: Peter Davies, 1947)

Morris, Ronald L.
Wait Until Dark: Jazz and the Underworld 1880-1940 (Bowling Green, Ohio: Bowling Green University Popular Press, 1980)

O'Day, Anita, with George Eells
High Times Hard Times (New York: Putnam, 1981 and London: Corgi, 1983)

Ostransky, Leroy
Jazz City: the Impact of Our Cities on the Development of Jazz (Englewood Cliffs, New Jersey: Prentice-Hall, 1978)

Philips, Cabell
From the Crash to the Blitz 1929-1939 (New York: Macmillan, 1969)

Placksin, Sally
American Women in Jazz (New York: Wideview, 1982)

Ramsey, Frederic, Jr., and Charles Edward Smith
Jazzmen (New York: Harcourt Brace, 1939 and London: Jazz Book Club, 1958)

Rozwenc, Edwin C.
The Making of American Society Volume II Since 1865 (Boston: Allyn and Bacon, 1973)

Sandburg, Carl
The Chicago Race Riots (New York: Harcourt, Brace and Howe, 1919)

Scott, Bobby
'Gene Krupa: The World Is Not Enough.' *Jazzletter*, 3, no. 6, January 1984. (Gene Lees, *Jazzletter*, Ojai, California.)

Shapiro, Nat and Nat Hentoff, eds.
Hear Me Talkin' to Ya: the Story of Jazz by the Men Who Made It (New York: Rinehart and London: Peter Davies, 1955)

Simon, George T.
The Big Bands (New York: Macmillan, 1971 and London:

	Collier Macmillan, 1974)
	Simon Says: the Sights and Sounds of the Swing Era 1935-1955 (New Rochelle: Arlington House, 1971)
Sinclair, Upton	*The Jungle* (London: Penguin, 1979)
Spaeth, Sigmund	*A History of Popular Music in America* (New York: Random House, 1948 and London: Phoenix House, 1960)
Spear, Allan H.	*Black Chicago: the Making of a Ghetto 1890-1920* (Chicago: University of Chicago Press, 1967)
Tuttle, William M.	*Race Riot* (New York: Atheneum, 1972)
Ulanov, Barry	*A Handbook of Jazz* (New York: Viking, 1957 and London: Hutchinson, 1958)
Waller, Maurice, and Anthony Calabrese	*Fats Waller* (London: Cassell, 1977)
Williams, Martin, ed.	*Jazz Panorama* (New York: Crowell 1964)

Articles in magazines and newspapers and sleeve notes to record albums by various writers including George Avakian, Bill Esposito, Mark Gardner, Alun Morgan, Arnold Shaw, John Shaw, George T. Simon, Steve Voce, Chris Welch, John S. Wilson, Michele Wood are mostly acknowledged in the main text. The journals include: *down beat, Esquire, Jazz and Blues, Jazz Journal International, Melody Maker, Metronome, The New York Times.* Record album sleeves include the Time-Life series, 'The Men Who Made the Music.'

INDEX

144